"The popular misconception that comic strip stories are easy to read, and therefore easy to write, is delightfully dispelled in Clive Brooks' and John Gatehouse's clear, informative and entertaining guide."

Jenny O'Connor,
Managing Editor, Marvel UK

The Way to Write Comics

CLIVE BROOKS
and
JOHN GATEHOUSE

Foreword by David Lloyd

Elm Tree Books . London

ELM TREE BOOKS

Published by the Penguin Group
27 Wrights Lane, London W8 5TZ, England
Viking Penguin Inc, 40 West 23rd Street, New York, New York 10010, U.S.A.
Penguin Books Australia Ltd, Ringwood, Victoria, Australia
Penguin Books Canada Ltd, 2801 John Street, Markham, Ontario, Canada L3R 1B4
Penguin Books (N.Z) Ltd, 182-190 Wairau Road, Auckland 10, New Zealand

Penguin Books Ltd, Registered Offices: Harmondsworth, Middlesex, England

First published in Great Britain 1988 by
Elm Tree Books

1 3 5 7 9 10 8 6 4 2

British Library Cataloguing in Publication Data

Brooks, Clive
The way to write comics. — (Way to
write).
1. Comics. Composition
I. Title   II. Gatehouse, John
III. Series
741.5

ISBN 0-241-12598-7
ISBN 0-241-12599-5 Pbk

Typeset by Pioneer, Perthshire.
Printed in Great Britain by
Billing and Sons Ltd, Guildford

Contents

for

MUM & DAD

for keeping me going when the going got tough!

John

for

my daughter, SOPHIE

(Born December 2nd, 1987)

Clive

Acknowledgements

We would like to give our thanks to John Royle, Jeff Short and Bambos Georgiou for all their efforts in producing the excellent pieces of artwork you will see in this book.

Also thanks to Geoff Willmetts for taking time to read through the first two chapters, suggesting improvements to the manuscript, and for his contributions to the Glossary of Comic Words.

We'd also like to thank Caroline Taggart for going along with our ideas for this book. It's nice to have an editor who lets us get on with the job without interference, and who always sounds cheerful — no matter what surprises we may spring on her!

Foreword

If you're the sort of person who thinks that writing for comics is going to be easy because they're just simple entertainment for children or second-rate literature for semi-illiterates, you'd better put this book down and find one on "Do-It-Yourself Brain Surgery" instead, because I don't want you writing comics for me or anyone else to draw. There are far too many unperceptive hacks in this business already and we can do without another one added to the list!

On the other hand, if you're one of those people who think that the blend of literature and art we call the Strip Cartoon is an exciting medium with a language of its own which is capable of unlimited expression, then the world of comics needs you greatly and I look forward to seeing your first story in print.

However, before you begin to learn "The Way to Write Comics", you'd better learn a few things about the way to treat comic artists. These wonderful people — of which I am one — will be turning your grand visions into grand pictures (or trying to) and they'll want some care and consideration taken over what you ask them to do so they don't have too many sleepless nights to cope with.

Firstly, above all, they need to have some *Creative Freedom* given to them. At all costs, resist the temptation to steer artists into following an exact pattern of scene description or picture composition, as if you were presenting a kind of Paint-by-Numbers design for them to work to. If you do this it will have the effect of totally intruding upon their creative 'territory' and will also give them the impression that you don't trust them to do the job properly without Step-by-Step instructions to cling to. Of course, there are some artists who are perfectly happy to take absolute guidance down to the last nut and bolt, but they're few and far between and certainly not common in the more highly-regarded areas of the business.

Secondly, wherever possible, give the artist some breathing space by supplying some relaxing areas of drawing to do. For instance, if it's not important for a certain scene to be set in the middle of a crowded street, with all the people and cars needing to be drawn, then indicate that it can be set anywhere else as long as it's appropriate. This will give the artist an opportunity to have a nice time drawing a favourite location as a backdrop — or something simple to depict, like a park or a beach.

A third point to bear in mind is that many experienced comic artists have drawn the same tired situations over and over again in their careers, I won't bore you with any here as I am sure you can imagine some for yourself. Most of them yearn to work on something that is more than just the complacently-produced cliche.

So, if you possibly can, give them the benefit of some extra effort in your inventiveness. Remember, it may take you only a *few minutes* at the typewriter to describe a scene you know is pretty boring, but the poor artist has to spend *hours* at the drawing board bringing it to some sort of life. At this early stage of your development — ie square one — that's all I feel comfortable suggesting you take note of in terms of care and consideration for the artist. However, I do have some advice to offer about looking after *yourself* as a craftsman and caring for the markets you work in.

I'll begin by saying that it's important to recognise that the general standard of writing in comics could be higher. This situation will alter when *you* burst upon the scene, of course, having learnt your skills from the dedicated study of this invaluable book; and I'm sure you'll join a growing band of excellent new writers (all taught by this book, naturally) who'll eventually raise standards in the business everywhere. This is all well and good.

However, it's not enough to just become terrific at writing what the current markets demand from you. It is also *absolutely essential* for you to push the accepted bounds of the medium — wherever this is possible — and to expand the area of its influence beyond its present audience. Recent years have seen some good examples of this kind of pioneering from people such as Raymond Briggs, Alan Moore, Frank Miller and Art Spiegelman; and their efforts have not only benefited their medium but have also, quite surprisingly, benefited them by bestowing widespread fame, success and financial reward. So often, in fields of creativity, excellent experiment and popular acclaim fail to go hand-in-hand; but now, in the extraordinary world of comics, they're doing so with increasing regularity.

If you can take a lesson from this and attempt to emulate these superb and successful craftsmen, you'll be doing exactly the right thing for yourself, the business and the craft of the comic strip: doing good for everyone and sacrificing nothing. The only thing you'll have to worry about then in terms of looking after yourself, is finding a good pension plan!

Finally, John wanted me to say something in this foreword about how I see the future of comics. It's clearly impossible to make any kind of prediction about the whole field because it's so variable in content. The most that can be done is to assess trends in various areas of the business, and even that is so open to many unforseeable factors that it's not really worth doing. The only useful option for me to take in attempting to address the subject is to say simply, and accurately, that it's all up to *you*! If you read this book carefully and apply all you learn from it, and take to heart all those pleas I've made for you to stretch your creative skills to their fullest, you stand a good chance of making the future of comics extremely bright and exciting. At the very least, you'll make it interesting and, certainly, solidly crafted.

Whatever you do, though, don't let me down and become just another hack. Do that and I'll be wishing *you'd* gone for that book on "Do-It-Yourself Brain Surgery", as well. . . .

David Lloyd
28th June 1988

Chapter One

Writing Comic Strips in Britain

Everybody knows what a comic is. We have all read them as children, and many people continue to read and collect comics in their adult life. If you're going to write for the comics, you need to know *exactly* what a comic strip is. Simply put, it is a story told in a sequence of narrative pictures. In bygone days, comic strips consisted of a sequence of illustrations in panels, with the story text shown underneath each panel.

In Britain, this changed with the arrival of *The Dandy* and *The Beano*, in the late Thirties. (Both of which are still going strong today!) Nowadays, except for stories aimed at children under-five, all comic strip stories are made up of the pictures and words incorporated into each panel of the story. The words are shown in captions, or in dialogue or 'think' balloons. But don't get the wrong idea. Just because they are called 'comics', doesn't mean that every story has to be funny. The term originated in the early days, when the strips were all humorous in content. Nowadays, there are just as many adventure and romance stories as there are humour strips.

In the 1970s, comics faced a bleak future. The pessimists predicted that there would be no comics in Britain by the end of the 1980s. There were many reasons for this. British business was in the doldrums, and the comics market mirrored this. Also, a lot of what was being produced was simply bad — uninspired, lacklustre, with no thought behind what was being produced. This continued into the '80s, with the threat of video and computer games competing with comics for the children's pocket money. But with the advent of the licensed series (see *Writing The Licensed Series*) and a new generation of creators who care about what they are producing, comics are on the upswing again. In the month that this chapter was written, there were 29 weekly comic titles published, ten fortnightly titles, and 21 monthly titles. There were also six Specials, or 'one-off' titles, which were published to gauge the readers' reaction. If these Specials sell, they will no doubt appear on a regular basis.

Of this number, there were 204 comic strips featured in the weekly titles alone (that is 204 strips *per week*!) of which, only five were reprinted material. There were also 14 text stories. (See: *Writing The Text Story*.) 33 strips appeared each fortnight, of which only four were reprints, and, if we do not include the monthly titles which were reprints, there were thirteen new strips in the monthly titles. So, not counting the 'Specials', in one month there were 270 comic strips, each requiring a writer!

Before you pop the champagne corks in celebration of this potential massive freelance market however, the truth is that many of the strips are written 'in-house', which means that they are created by someone on the staff of a comic company. A good number of other strips have been written for a number of months or years by a regular, established writer, who would not appreciate relinquishing 'their' strip to a newcomer. And, especially nowadays, companies are also bringing out comics that feature reprinted material, for which they do not have to pay. (This is true of many of the monthly titles from Fleetway, where an entire title can be made up of reprinted stories.) Your best chance is to find a strip which does not have a regular writer (this you can find out by writing to the editor of the comic concerned), or by creating your own character and series to sell to a comic.

How many strips does a comic contain? There's no easy answer. It can be anything between one and 22, though the majority have fewer than ten strips. More than this, and the comic will definitely be humour-orientated, with many strip series only running for one page. Other comic strips run for as many as ten pages. These are generally stories featured in the adventure titles for boys.

Nowadays, a great number of titles appear in full colour throughout. Of the others, most feature at least four pages in colour. This varies from company to company, with Marvel Comics and London Editions using colour in all their titles, while Fleetway and D. C. Thomson still produce most of their strips in black and white. (In America, all the main-stream companies use colour throughout their comic range.) Generally, it makes little difference to the writer whether a strip appears in colour or black and white, though occasionally a writer will use one or other of the formats to the advantage of the story. Black and white is useful for producing a gothic feel to a horror story, while colour can bring life to the 'verdant alien paradise planet' a writer has created in his script.

Many people are under the misconception that comic strips are written and drawn by the same person. The truth is that each job requires different skills. It is unusual in Britain to find a creator who is adept at both writing and drawing. (In America, there are a number of famous comic strip writer-artists.) Since you've bought this book we assume it's your comic writing skills that you want to develop.

The difference between writing text-fiction, and writing the comic strip, is that with text-fiction you use words to form picture images in a reader's mind, whereas with the comic strip you write words *for* pictures.

When you decide to write for comics you become one member of a team, consisting of an editor, a writer, an artist, (in some cases, more so in America, this may consist of two people, a penciller and an inker), a letterer, and, (if the story is going to appear in colour), a colourist. Each of these people play an important role in the creation of a comic strip. If you are going to work in comics you should have some idea of what each person does.

The Editor has full control of each strip. He or she will decide which writers and artists to use on a strip series. If you haven't yet had anything published, it's often a good idea to send an introductory letter, submitting details of any story ideas you have, or even a full unsolicited script. If your work is already known, you may receive a 'phone call from an editor asking whether you would like to work on a new strip for their comic.

In fact, a number of editors now prefer writers, even established writers, to submit a synopsis of a story before they write up a script. This synopsis can be anything between one or two sentences to a full page, and allows for any necessary changes to be made before a full script is drawn up. This is to the benefit of both the editor and writer. It is up to you to find out what is required.

The Artist is the person who will interpret your directions and turns your written script into a panel-by-panel comic strip. They may keep exactly to your script or use it as a guideline. Experienced artists are able to visualise an idea better than most writers, and often make changes to improve the overall look of a poor script.

The Letterer's job is to copy any narrative and dialogue indicated in the script, and to judge where best to place it in a panel, without obscuring the artwork.

The Colourist, (if one is required), colours in the black and white photocopies of the artist's pictures.

By the time your script has passed through all these hands it may look very different from what you had originally imagined. These people are professionals in their field, and the editor doesn't make changes to a script without valid reasons. They've been in the business long enough to know how to turn a weak script into a strong one!

The writer is an important link in this creative chain. Without a writer there is no story, and so no comic strip. Editors respect a writer who can produce perfect scripts every time within the deadlines available. If you are just starting out this may sound hard to believe, but with practice, you can reach this stage easily.

Comic strips have many similarities to film and television scripts, and are written in much the same way. You, the writer, must give information in your script relating to scene directions, and ensure that it's clear who is speaking. The advantage of the comic strip is that you can be as imaginative as you want, using as many special effects as your story requires, without it costing a fortune. Artists can draw a planet exploding just as easily as they can draw two people standing in a field. (This does not, of course, mean that every story requires flashy special effects. Often, a subdued approach is just as effective.)

Firstly, decide on the type of story you want to write. The advantage of British comics is that there is a range of topics to choose from. (In America, the super hero rules supreme!) All subject preferences are catered for. You can choose between humour, adventure, sport, romance, war, science

4

fiction, historical dramas, licensed character series, horror, super heroes, fairy tale stories for the very young, thrillers and crime. Somewhere in that list is a story suited to your abilities as a writer.

A professional writer can write about all of these subjects. But to start with, choose a subject that you feel most comfortable with. The only subject that is not covered in this list is westerns. Western stories used to be incredibly popular, especially in the Fifties, but have been overtaken by the more imaginative subject of science fiction, and there is now little call for western stories in British comics. This is not to say you will never sell a western story, but the story would have to be very good to stand any chance of getting past an editor.

If you are any good at writing comedy, the best market for you is the humour comics. While most titles have an occasional one or two page humour strip, there are specific humour-orientated titles on sale, such as *Buster* (Fleetway), *The Beano* (D. C. Thomson) and *Mad* (Suron). Most are marketed for the seven to eleven age group, though *Mad*, and Fleetway's *Oink* comic, tend to have an older teenage/adult readership. The page rate (how much you are paid for each page of script) won't give you many luxury holidays — unless you are very prolific — but then you are only required to write one, or at most, two, pages of a story. This will give you the opportunity to decide whether comic script writing is suited to you, without wasting too much time and effort.

Except in titles aimed at the teenage market, the humour in these stories is diluted, and suitable for a young audience. There is no room for suggestive, or rude jokes. The humour tends to revolve around safe, bland, slapstick routines, with the principal character usually getting on top of the bullies or baddies by the end of the eleven or 21 panel story. The only exception is when the lead character is naughty or mischievous, and they sometimes come off second-best against teachers and parents. Social conscience has even infiltrated comics. Once, a mischievous lead character might have ended a story receiving the cane or the slipper — but nowadays, it is safer for a writer to find some other way to give these characters their 'just deserts'.

Basically, there are two ways to write up a comic strip

script for British comics. The first is the layout used by the majority of the companies, and the second is a variation required by only one of the British companies, London Editions. We'll look at this shortly.

To start with you must create a plot for a story. It is best to write your ideas down in rough, on a spare sheet of paper. When you are more experienced, you'll find that you can create plots, and calculate exactly how many panels a story will need, in your head. But to start with, it is better to keep notes of your ideas. The following rough plot synopsis will give you a guide as to how much space you have to tell your story. Remember, if a comic only requires a specific number of panels to a story, you cannot exceed this. An eleven panel story means just that. If you wish to use a bigger or smaller panel for special effect, or require an extra panel to tell your story, an editor will sometimes allow this, but it is best to keep to the number of panels stated, especially if you are just starting out. After all, you must show that you can write a story in the room available. If you write a story that needs sixteen panels, your script is likely to be returned as unsuitable.

The layout of a comic strip causes unnecessary worry for new writers. Editors receive many strange-looking scripts, that have to be consigned to that circular filing cabinet on the floor, simply because they are not laid out in the required manner. This includes scripts that have been written as if they were short text stories, and other scripts that have been written by hand or on both sides of a piece of paper. However good a story may be, unless it is presented in the proper format for comic scripts, it will not stand a chance of selling to an editor. So make it easy on yourself, and do the job right first time out.

All scripts must be typed double spaced, (leaving an extra blank line between each typed line) using one side of a sheet of A4 paper only. At least one inch should be left for margins on both sides of the text, and at the top and bottom of the page. This is to allow editors to make corrections, or to give specific instructions to the artist. All pages must be numbered.

At the top left of each page of your script write your name. To the right of this write either the title of the series you are scripting, or the story title. This is in case the pages of your script become separated in the confusion of an editor's office. (Editors are always in a state of confusion!) Three or four spaces below this, write the title of the series, and a double space below this, write the story title, if there is one. Both should be centred in the page.

So, for example:

Creative Imaginations   **Jester**

Jester
Jester's Japes

Leave two double spaces below this. Then on the left, write the number 1. This tells the artist that this is panel 1. (Some writers actually write PANEL 1. It is not necessary, but if you feel happier doing this, go right ahead!)

Indent three spaces from the panel number. If you are starting your story with a caption (to describe a certain time or place, i.e. SOON, LATER or, IN THE THRONE ROOM . . .) then write CAP: and the short passage you wish to write. (Captions, dialogue and sound effects are written in CAPITAL LETTERS.) Keep the captions short and simple, and only use them when changing scenes in a story.

Double spaced below the caption, write the artist's directions. This is where you become a bit like a film director, but instead of giving directions to the camera, you are telling the artist what visual requirements are needed in the panel.

It is up to you to describe what is happening in the panel. All art directions are written in lower case letters. Depending on the type of story, you may be able to give just a basic outline: e.g.:

In King Arthur's throne room. Jester gives King Arthur a hearty slap on the back. He slaps him so hard Arthur's teeth shoot out of his mouth.

Or, you may need to give precise details of what should be drawn in the panel: e.g.:

7

Large panel. Sarah and Julie are running out of school, *Greendean Comprehensive*, through the large double gates. Both girls are aged about 11, and wear smart school uniforms. Sarah carries a satchel over her shoulder, which swings behind her as she runs. Sarah has blonde, long, flowing hair, while Julie's is permed. Sarah is smiling, but Julie looks glum. In the background, other boys and girls of different ages are seen. A flashy sports car is parked on the opposite side of the street. Sitting in the driver's seat is a young man, about twenty, with a thin moustache. He wears a sports jacket, and a smart pair of sunglasses.

The type of story you are writing dictates how much detail is required in a script. While we have mentioned that Sarah is blonde and describe the girls hair styles, other writers would not have bothered with such descriptions, and left it up to the discretion of the artist. We add such descriptions for the benefit of the artist, and for ourselves, to help create an image of the characters in our minds. But don't overdo it. When giving art directions, don't forget the poor artist. He can only draw a certain amount of information in a panel.

Amateur scriptwriters tend to fill panels to capacity with characters and happenings. Imagine being an artist on the receiving end of this instruction:

An army of one thousand warriors, on horseback, on the horizon. Each warrior is dressed in full armour, and carrying lances and swords. One warrior sits on his horse playing the bagpipes. The warrior behind him is finishing a half-eaten apple. A maggot can be seen poking its head out of the side of the apple. In the foreground, there is a village of fifteen wooden huts. Children are playing leapfrog in a clearing. Women are sitting outside each hut. Give each woman a different dress. A dog is tied to a post outside one hut, scratching its ear. To the left of the picture ten men are in the field, sowing bags of seed. In the sky above, three birds fly overhead. . . . . . '.

We made up this art direction, but editors have received much worse. No wonder artists grumble about some comic writers! If your story really needs 'an army of thousands' then imply the army exists in the captions, while asking the artist to show only two or three of the warriors, at most. Always take the artist's restrictions into consideration. They'll love you for it, and may even ask to work on one of your scripts again!

Below the art directions, write the dialogue the characters will speak. Dialogue is placed in 'dialogue balloons', (sometimes called 'speech balloons'). These indicate which character is speaking. As a good rule of thumb, remember that the maximum number of words you should have to one balloon is twenty-five. There is an obvious practical reason for keeping speech short and simple: if you write too much dialogue in one panel, the letterer will have problems fitting in his balloons without covering up important aspects of the artwork. For the same reason, never have more than two characters speaking in one panel.

For example:
JESTER: GOOD MORNING, SIRE!
KING ARTHUR: OOF! ME TEESH!

or:

SARAH: YIPPEE! NO MORE ROTTEN SCHOOL FOR SIX GLORIOUS WEEKS. DAD'S TAKING US FOR A CRUISE DOWN THE RHINE IN HIE NEW YACHT!
JULIE: HUH! I CAN'T EVEN AFFORD TO GO TO BUTLINS!

The advantage of comics is that we can see what the characters are thinking, as well as speaking. Instead of having Julie speaking in example two, we could have asked the letterer to place her words in a thought balloon, i.e.

JULIE (thinks): HUH! I CAN'T EVEN AFFORD TO GO TO BUTLINS!

There is one other requirement when writing a comic strip, and that is the use of onomatopoeia — imitative sound words, or sound effects, such as KRRRRAAAASSSSH! BLATT! BLOIP! ZAP! SPLOOTT! FIBBEDY FLUPPP! HA HA HARR!! These are generally used to best effect in humour and adventure stories. They are great fun to create. (See *Guide To Comic Words*.) These 'Sound Effects' or 'Special Effects' (SFX) are usually placed before dialogue in the scripts, and always in CAPITALS. So, if we go back to the example of JESTER, the completed directions up to the end of panel 1 would look like this:

Creative Imaginations   **Jester**

Jester
Jester's Japes

1.   CAP: IN THE THRONE ROOM . . .

In King Arthur's throne room. Jester gives King Arthur a hearty slap on the back. Jester slaps him so hard Arthur's teeth shoot out of his mouth.

SLAAAP!
JESTER: GOOD MORNING, SIRE!
KING ARTHUR: OOF! ME TEESH!

You continue in exactly the same way throughout the script until you come to the end of your story. It is worth mentioning that panel numbering is run in a continuous sequence, no matter how many pages of the comic strip there are. For example, page one of the strip may feature panels one to seven. Page two will continue this panel count with panels eight to fifteen, etc. After the last art direction, leave two spaces and write 'ends', centred beneath. And that's all there is to it. Easy, isn't it?

JESTER SCRIPT

1. In the throne room of King Arthur's castle. Jester, dressed in the old fashioned clothes of a court jester, slaps King Arthur on the back. He slaps him so hard that the King's teeth shoot out of his mouth.

JESTER: HELLO, SIRE!
KING ARTHUR: OOFFF! ME TEESH!

2. Sir Prancelot, dressed in a suit of armour, with only his head showing, sniggers at the notice pinned on Arthur's back. It reads I'M A TWIT. Jester giggles, rolling on the ground.

PRANCELOT: HA HA! JESTER, CAUGHT YOU OUT WITH THAT OLD JOKE, SIRE!
KING ARTHUR: SERVE MY TEA, PRANCELOT. YOUR JOKES GET WORSE, JESTER!

3. Sitting at the big round table are King Arthur and Jester. On the table there are bowls of trifle and cakes. Jester passes a cake on a plate to King Arthur.

JESTER: HAVE A CAKE, SIRE.
KING ARTHUR: THANKS, JESTER.

4. King Arthur takes a big bite of the cake, and a jet of ink spurts into his face. Jester laughs. Prancelot's armour squeaks as he tries not to burst out laughing.

SPLUURTT!
SQUEAK! SQUEAK!

JESTER: "CAKE THAT", SIRE! HAW! HAW!
KING ARTHUR: GLOOP!

5. LATER . . .
   It's night time, we can see the moon through one of the long slit windows of the castle. Prancelot is still dressed in his armour, but now, there's a nightshirt over the top of it.

12

He's wearing a little nightcap on his head, and is carrying a candle in a holder to light his way. Jester sticks his leg out for Prancelot to trip over.

PRANCELOT: YAWN! I'M BUSHED! WHOOPSIES!
JESTER: HAVE A GOOD TRIP! HAW HAW!

6. Big sound effect:

KERRRAASSSHHH!!

7. The battered Prancelot and King Arthur whisper together in the darkened round tower. Arthur is dressed similar to Prancelot in nightshirt and little cap — but without the armour.

KING ARTHUR: THAT JESTER'S GETTING TO BE A PAIN!
PRANCELOT: OUCH! YOU'RE RIGHT, SIRE! LET'S GET OUR OWN BACK!

8. SO . . .
   Jester is in his nightshirt in his castle bedroom. He jumps into his bed.

JESTER: HO HUM! TIME FOR BED!

9. Jester leaps out of bed, high into the air, and shoots out through the open castle window. Stuck to his bottom is a sharp-pointed helmet, as worn by knights.

JESTER: YEEEOOOWWCCCHHH!

10. OUTSIDE . . .
   Jester lands in the moat.

SPLOOSSHH!!

11. King Arthur and Prancelot stand at the bank in the moonlight, looking at the drenched Jester sitting in the moat with a frog on his head.

KING ARTHUR: AS A JESTER YOU'RE ALL WASHED
UP!
PRANCELOT: WE MADE A BIG SPLASH WITH OUR
JOKE! HA! HA! HA!
JESTER: BAH!

We mentioned that the layout of a script for London
Editions differs slightly from those for other companies. The
changes are small, but they are worth remembering. The
company deals specifically with publishing comic titles based
on licensed characters. (See *Writing The Licensed Series*.)

When Brian Clarke took over the editorial reins at London
Editions, he decided to create a standard script format, for
two reasons. First, many of the writers who work for the
company are new to the comic market, and he wanted to
force them to think in terms of visuals before they wrote any
captions or dialogue. London Editions also uses a number of
European artists, whose native language is not English, and
who require scripts that spell everything out clearly.
Therefore, you must write all directions in full. Instead of
just numbering a panel, you *must* write PANEL 1, PANEL 2,
etc, in CAPITALS. Other directions, such as 'action' and
'dialogue', must also be written in full, but in lower case
letters. All character names, when discussed in the art
directions, are shown in CAPITALS.

Using one of our own original series we show an example
of the type of script layout London Editions require. (The
number in brackets after the series title represents the page
number of the script.):

TIDAL FORCE (3)   CREATIVE IMAGINATIONS
PANEL 8
action
Long shot showing TIDAL FORCE and DOCTOR DECAY
battling over the skyscrapers of New York. A blast of 'hard
water' shoots from one of TIDAL FORCE's hands. The blast
strikes DOCTOR DECAY, sending him hurtling across the
sky.

caption
TIDAL FORCE DREW UPON THE MOISTURE OF THE
AIR TO INCREASE HIS STRENGTH!

dialogue
Tidal Force
YOUR EVIL HAS DESTROYED THE LIVES OF HUN-
DREDS OF INNOCENT PEOPLE! NOW FEEL MY
POWER!
Doctor Decay
YAAAAGGH!

noises (Extra large letters)
ZAAAM!

The 'noises' are another term for Sound Effects. Words that
need to be emphasised are underlined in the script as a guide
to the letterer.

Photo-Stories

There is another type of strip that is popular in Britain, but
only in the teenage romance titles. This is the photo-story.
As its name suggests, these strips are told through photographs instead of illustrations. This imposes certain limitations
on the writer. Exotic locations and imaginative visuals cannot
be considered. The photographer has a small budget. He
can't afford to spend time setting up mock backgrounds for
new worlds, or travel to a specific type of building, like
Buckingham Palace!

When writing the photo-story, the rule is to keep it simple.
Since the majority of stories involve young love, and its
many pitfalls, stories that revolve around school, night clubs
or the home, are best. Do not involve too many characters in
the stories. Live models need to be paid for their time, and a
script that requires a 'hundred dancing girls', will not be
considered by a budget-conscious editor. This example of a
teenage romance story 'Sweet Music' could also be adapted
to a photo-story.

SWEET MUSIC

1. Caption: MUM HATES MY RECORDS . . .

Judy's mum is poking her head around Judy's bedroom door, shouting at the top of her voice. The bedroom walls are covered in posters. Records are strewn across the floor. A record player is blaring out in the corner.

Judy's Mum: TURN THAT ROW DOWN. CAN'T YOU FIND SOME SENSIBLE HOBBY TO KEEP YOU OCCUPIED.

Judy: (thinks): HUH, LIKE WHAT?

2. Caption: ON THE WAY TO SCHOOL . . .

Judy is upstairs on the school bus gazing out of the window into a local music shop. Two of her friends are sitting opposite.

Carol: JUDY'S DREAMING AGAIN. I WONDER WHO IT IS THIS TIME?

Sharon: MR NOBODY PROBABLY, SHE'S NEVER HAD A REAL BOYFRIEND.

3. Same frame, Judy looks down thoughtfully.

Judy: (thinks): THEY'RE RIGHT, I NEVER GO ANYWHERE TO MEET ANYONE. BUT MUM'S SUGGESTION COULD CHANGE THAT.

4. Caption: AT LUNCHTIME . . .

Judy is in a phonebox near the school. She looks nervous as she makes a call.

Judy: H-HELLO, I'D LIKE TO BOOK SOME GUITAR LESSONS, BUT I'VE NEVER PLAYED BEFORE.

Voice (from the phone): THAT'S ALL RIGHT. COME ALONG AT SEVEN O'CLOCK TONIGHT, I'LL SOON GET YOU GOING.

5. Caption: THAT EVENING . . .

Judy arrives at the door of the teaching studio. The door is half open and we see the face of a good looking boy in the doorway.

Boy: HELLO JUDY, COME IN, I'M DAVE THE TUTOR.

Judy: (embarrassed) OH, UH, T-THANKS.

Judy: (thinks) GOSH, HE'S REALLY GOOD LOOKING, AND NOT MUCH OLDER THAN ME EITHER.

6.

Judy and Dave are sitting on chairs in a classroom. Judy has a guitar on her lap. Dave is holding Judy's hand in the correct position on the guitar neck. Judy is trying not to giggle.

Dave: WE'LL START WITH THIS MAJOR CHORD.

Judy: (thinks): MM, THIS IS MORE FUN THAN I THOUGHT.

7. Caption: A FEW WEEKS LATER

Scene in the classroom at school. Carol has snatched Judy's schoolbook from her and is looking at the graffitti filled cover with Sharon. Judy is looking on in annoyance.

Carol: WHO'S THIS DAVE, WRITTEN ALL OVER YOUR BOOK THEN?

Judy: MIND YOUR OWN BUSINESS AND GIVE IT BACK.

8.

Same scene. Judy has got her book back. She is facing the camera, clutching it to her and smiling. Sharon and Carol are laughing behind their hands in the background.

Judy: (thinks) DAVE'S BOUND TO ASK ME OUT SOON. I'LL SHOW HIM OFF TO THOSE TWO CREEPS WHEN HE DOES. THAT'LL SHUT THEM UP.

9. Caption: AFTER SCHOOL . . .

Judy has just arrived back home after school. The scene is the kitchen. Her mum is at the sink doing some washing up. Judy is standing behind her.

Judy: I NEED SOME EXTRA POCKET MONEY, MUM. I'VE STARTED GUITAR LESSONS, AND I WANT SOME EXTRA TUITION. CAN I DO SOME JOBS AROUND THE HOUSE?

Judy's Mum: OF COURSE. IT MAKES A CHANGE FOR YOU TO TAKE MY ADVICE.

10. Caption: JUDY'S PESTERED DAVE FOR WEEKS. HE'S GETTING FED UP WITH HER . . .

Dave is standing in his teaching studio talking to a friend.

Dave: SHE'S ALWAYS BOOKING EXTRA TUITION. I KNOW IT'S BECAUSE SHE FANCIES ME, BUT I DON'T WANT TO HURT HER.

Friend: WHY DON'T YOU TELL HER THAT THERE'S NOTHING MORE TO LEARN. THAT'LL GET RID OF HER.

Dave: GREAT IDEA!

Photo-story scripts are laid out exactly like a comic strip. Dialogue rather than action moves the story along. Indicate to the photographer exactly what you wish to convey in a panel. It is best to limit the number of characters to a panel to two or three, if at all possible. If you get on well with teenagers and feel you can communicate with them on their level this could be the type of comic writing you are best suited for.

Young Children

The types of comic strip we have already discussed are aimed at older children and teenagers. The third type is aimed at the under-fives. A block of text is printed beneath each panel of artwork. The text is simple, and contains a maximum of 30 words per panel. Many companies now require the writer to count the exact number of characters of each word of a panel. You will find this time-consuming, and often frustrating. It is not always easy to find the right words with the exact number of characters needed to fill the restricted block of text. When writing the script, the text is shown first, followed by the art directions. Here is an example from THE GORILLA FAMILY (for a full specimen page of script and artwork see *Writing The Licensed Series*):

1. LITTLE RODNEY GORILLA PICKED UP HIS BUCKET AND SPADE. "I'M GOING TO BUILD A SANDCASTLE!" HE GIGGLED.

ART: Rodney Gorilla is sitting on the beach with a bucket and spade. It's a sunny day, and he's near the sea shore.

Some editors prefer the story text on one sheet of paper and the art directions on another. Ask an editor what they want, before you write up that story!

Now that you know how to lay out a comic script, let's consider specific problems. How many panels should you have to a page? How many panels and pages to a story? How many characters should be featured in a panel?

The answers to these questions come from a detailed

study of the market. Before writing anything, you should read at least four issues of the comic you want to write for. You will then get the feel of the type of story an editor is looking for.

It is difficult to give strict guidelines on the number of pages, (or panels) required for a story. Humour stories tend to run for 10 to 11 panels to each page of story. Strips for the under-five's will have approximately four to six panels per page, and may run to as many as five pages. Adventure and photo stories have six to 10 panels each page, and the stories can range from three to 12 pages.

Research

Research is a must. When studying a comic, ask yourself these questions:

* What audience is the comic aimed at? Girls? Boys? Mixed?
* What is the average age of the readership? (You can tell the age group by the type of stories and the advertisements that are featured in the comic.)
* Which subjects appear to be taboo, and why? Comics have to be careful not to upset parents or pressure groups. In the past, comics have been criticised as having a bad effect on children. Even today, certain titles are criticised in the 'popular' press when journalists haven't anything better to do. However, comics have proved to be of use in teaching children to read. They're also an entertainment media, on a par with television and films. Even so, editors are careful not to publish any controversial material. (Sex, gratuitous violence, drugs — including glue-sniffing — and smoking must never be depicted in a children's comic.
* What trends are in favour? (When skateboards, CB radio, and breakdancing, were in fashion, there were comic strips to accompany them.)
* How many characters are featured per story, and how many characters are shown in each panel?
* How much dialogue is used? How many words to each speech balloon?
* Are sound effects used in the stories?

The answers to these questions will help you in the writing of a script for a specific comic. When you have had experience of writing comic strips, you will find you know the answers automatically. But if you are just starting out, research is all-important.

Chapter Two

How to Structure a Comic Strip Story

Now that you understand how comic strip scripts are laid out, it is worth spending a chapter discussing what is required in the stories themselves. What are the ingredients that make up a comic story? How do you use them to the best advantage? Can you write a story without them? We can find the answers to these questions by breaking down a script piece by piece:

Plot

What is a plot? That sounds a silly question, but you would be surprised at the number of amateur writers who are stumped for an answer. A plot is simply a plan of action. It is the base from which the story gradually develops through the unfolding of a connected series of incidents. The drama element comes from the needs, hopes and dreams of the characters, and how they set about reaching their goals. You need to sit down and work out a series of inter-connecting events that will lead to the end result — the explosive climax.

Keep your plots simple. You'll usually be writing for an audience of children, whose attention span is short-lived. If the story they are reading is full of convoluted plots that are hard to follow, they will turn the page to the next story. That is proof of failure to a writer. One good idea and conflict is all that is needed for the majority of comic stories. So throw away any ideas that seem too complicated, or better still, keep them in your files, until you come to the time when you want to write that 'blockbuster' novel!

The best stories are written on the basis of cause and effect. This is best described as someone taking a course of action: to start up a football team, rob a bank, or ask out a pretty girl, for instance. This is cause. The effect comes from what occurs as a result of the action the person decides to take. The incidents need to be related, otherwise they do not form a plot. They are simply a series of casual, or accidental events, with no relationship to one another. If, however, something happens — *Tidal Force* battles with *Doctor Decay* — as a direct result of something else that has happened — *Doctor Decay* has poisoned the girlfriend of *Tidal Force* and only he holds the antidote — then you have the makings of a plot.

You can't begin to write a story without a well-constructed plot to start you off. It doesn't matter where your plot originates — it can even be from a word of phrase that flashes into your head — but from then on, it's important to expand this 'itch' of an idea into a fully developed storyline — the plot.

Whenever you write a plot, ask yourself the following questions:

* Exactly who is the lead character? (Our hero! He has to be someone who stands out from the crowd.)
* What is he trying to accomplish? What does he have to sacrifice to attain his goals? (All heroes make sacrifices! It helps to show their noble spirit!)
* Who, or what, is his adversary? (It doesn't have to be someone downright evil — though such characters are always more fun to write! — but a character who has similar, or different goals to the lead character. A character who is the opposite, in wants and needs, to Our hero.)
* What troubles does he face along the way? (Your character may be unable to save his girlfriend because he's too busy saving the lives of thousands of innocent bystanders.
* What action will he take? (The character shouldn't wait around for someone else to sort out the mess. He should take direct action, based on his knowledge and abilities.)
* What happens from the action he takes? (This is where you can be nasty and make life hard for him — hey, no one said the life of a Hero was easy! Perhaps his decision was the wrong one. Or, his actions were right, but they have created a new problem or threat.)

* Can things get any worse? (Yes! Make his life uncomfortable. The time when everything seems hopeless, he could just give up. It may be more realistic, but it's not a very satisfying conclusion to a story.)
* How does the story end? (And it must, eventually. Comics prefer a climax that shows the true conquering spirit of the lead character, where he wins through in the face of overwhelming odds. Show the character attaining his goals, succeeding in what he set out to do. Popularly known as the happy ending. Of course, you can have the Unhappy Ending. Whichever is more suited to the consequences of the character's actions — and whether you're in a bad mood that day!)

Also remember that no permanent change is allowed in the life of the leading character, unless permission is first granted by an editor. So, for instance, if you have a story where the hero is found to be suffering from a crippling disease that threatens to take away the use of his legs, the story must conclude with the character making a full recovery. And that is really all there is to creating the plot.

Where do plot ideas come from? Everywhere and everything! Newspaper and magazine stories are a good source for the writer. Create a file to keep newspaper items that catch your eye. Television and books are full of successful ideas which you may be able to adapt to the needs of a comic strip. Pictures in art galleries, or even on greeting cards may be the trigger you need to set off a plot. Your ideas may be sparked off from something ordinary: a child playing marbles in the street, a car running through a red light, someone taking their dirty clothes into a laundrette.

Exploring the last idea further, we could use this as a plot for a teenage romance story. Jill, a girl of about seventeen, has to take her washing to the laundrette because the washing machine at home has broken down. We can create conflict in our story by suggesting that she must have her clothes cleaned and pressed quickly because she has a job interview that afternoon.

This is not enough of a story on its own. Since this is a romance story let's add a handsome young man, who Jill bumps into in the street outside the laundrette. This is Tony, someone Jill has fancied, but hasn't had the nerve to talk to. This is a second source of conflict. Tony is too full of his own self-importance to talk to Jill. To give the story an added twist, when Jill gets back home the engineer has arrived to fix the washing machine. He is Jill's age, an apprentice. He looks scruffy, and is not that good-looking. Jill doesn't give him a second thought.

This may not sound like much substance for a story. But with a little thought we can have Jill, as the story progresses, realise that Tony is a right pig, (especially if he works at the firm Jill has a job interview with, and is the cause of Jill not being chosen) while the apprentice engineer turns out to be a 'knight in shining armour'. To add humour to our story, our 'knight' can be tarnished. He is inept as an engineer, causing the washing machine in Jill's kitchen to flood. While he is mopping up the mess Jill begins to realise that while he is accident-prone, he is more human than Tony could ever be. If you think you can develop a story from this, by all means, be our guest!

We should mention that comics are still deplorably sexist in many ways, though many editors are sure to disagree! Matters have improved in some areas, but girls are still looked on as weak and helpless, while boys are indoctrinated to believe that males are meant to be macho, and rarely show fear. This is why adventure comics are aimed specifically at boys, romance titles at girls, and humour titles at both sexes. While a boy character may do something brave, like fighting off a horde of alien invaders, a girl character is likely to get upset, because she has to miss meeting her boyfriend at the disco, due to having to babysit her brother! There are occasional role-reversals, but not enough in our opinion. There are also few, if any, coloured leading characters in comic strips. In this respect, British comics still exist in the Dark Ages!

Characters

All comic stories need good, solid characters to make the stories work. You will find that plots come from the characters themselves. Before writing a story, you must get to know your characters, otherwise your story will be weak, no matter how good the plot may be. Good characterisation is all-important to a story.

The lead character should always motivate the action. Your character should be seen to do something, in an effort to achieve his goals. He must be in the forefront of the story at all times, not waiting for something to happen. Through the story the character should be seen to develop as a person. He should be seen to change, to learn something about himself, and to become a better person for his experience. This really only applies to stories where there is room for development. But even in the one page humour strip, it is possible to develop a character in small ways. A character who hates going to school can discover that it's better than being stuck at home all day, bored.

The lead characters of children's comics strips do not have to be children. But when children are used, they should be incorporated into a story realistically, not for the sake of having a child character. It would be unrealistic to have a child piloting an aeroplane, except in extreme circumstances, but it would be in keeping for a child to collect aeroplane numbers, and for the story to flow from this.

Are your characters strong-willed, jealous, proud, conceited, nervous, evil, or funny? How do they express themselves? Have they got their own type of 'slang' speech, do they speak clearly, or with a 'plum in their mouth'?!

Dropping a syllable from a word — 'dyin', cryin', talkin', etc. is a useful speech device, and well-used in comics, which prefer shortened versions of words where possible. 'Can't', 'won't', 'shan't', are always employed by the writer, rather than the full word. Remember, we only have a certain amount of room for words in a 'speech balloon'. Dialogue should sound natural, but used clearly and economically. Listen to the way children talk, and study the current popular phrases. Although abbreviated words are used, English should be kept within the bounds of readability. Swearing is not allowed, except for the occasional 'blast', though you can use funny appropriate swearing, e.g.: "furballs!" or "buttercups!"! Dialogue must move the story along and reveal the characters innermost feelings to a reader. The beauty of comics is that characters may speak, even if they are not featured in the panel that their speech balloon appears in. When you want to use this device make sure the letterer knows the character is speaking, 'off-panel'.

In the comic strip story, only use those characteristics which are relevant. Remember, a comic strip is a short story told in pictures, so there is no room for unnecessary information, unless it has some bearing on the story. Our own character, JESTER, may enjoy hang-gliding in his nightgown on Sunday afternoons at three o'clock, but this has little bearing on our sample story, so we don't need to mention it. (Of course, we could always keep this idea on file for a future story!). It is important to focus on the main event of the story, and not to allow the story to wander in different directions.

Visualising your Story

Comic strips need careful thought when writing. They're a static medium. Unlike television or films, your characters don't move. Scripts from inexperienced writers suffer from recurring faults: they try to show each moment of time, and each movement of a character, in a story. You don't need to show a character waking up, brushing his teeth, having breakfast, packing his briefcase, walking down the road, catching the bus, and arriving at the office to start work. This is dull and tedious writing. Far better to use one caption: NEXT MORNING, ALAN ARRIVED AT WORK . . . to explain what is going on. If your story requires an indication of the passage of time, take advantage of captions and dialogue to do this.

Your job is to tell a well-structured story through the use of pictures. Each picture must carry the story forward. All stories should begin with a picture and dialogue that immediately captures the reader's attention and entices them to read on. Everybody says this, but it really *is* like writing a film script. In our case, we have to choose from a selection of 'stills', (panels of artwork), to tell our story.

Scriptwriting requires much thought and skill. The writer must consider how best to start the story, and how it should be developed along the way. Exercise your imagination, and make full use of the dramatic situations that your characters find themselves in. Break down a story into a beginning, a middle and an end, then divide this by the number of panels you have, and work out how many panels you will require for each part. You must be flexible, middles tend to need more space than beginnings and endings. A story should be sewn up immediately after its resolution. One or two panels should be all you need to round a story off!

Action

All comic stories need action. This doesn't have to be of the violent kind, though a certain amount is indispensible in boys adventure stories. Action is best described as something which happens to further the narrative. Action scenes which bear no relation to the plot are useless.

Conflict and Suspense

Whatever type of story you write, conflict and suspense are necessary. The lead character must face adversity before reaching his or her goals. Only through conflict is drama built up in a story. You must always give the impression that the character may not win through. A good story creates an atmosphere of anxiety, to keep the reader on the edge of their seat. If you give away too much information, or create a weak opponent for the lead character, the conclusion of the story will become obvious long before the final panels.

Build up the obstacles facing Our Hero. Make each one more difficult than the last, so that he must give more than his best effort to win through. He must surmount overwhelming odds to accomplish his goals, triumphing by the skin of his teeth! It goes without saying, that the problems and obstacles that he faces should be a natural extension of his actions, not created to suit you simply because you can't be bothered to put some effort into your thinking! To keep the story exciting, unexpected developments are needed, hopefully to the surprise of the reader. These story twists may create further conflict and suspense, but again, they must be a natural extension of the plot, not merely stuck in to keep a story from flagging. Side plots should not distract from the main plot. If they are that good, keep them for another time, to be made into a story in their own right.

Emotion

All characters need emotion to flesh out their personalities. Everyone has experienced the emotions of love, hate, fear, envy, guilt, pride, self-pity, vanity, despair. Emotion brings characters to life, affecting the reader, and drawing them deeper into the story.

Setting

Readers will soon become bored if a comic strip remains static: scenes should be constantly viewed from different angles. Or a different location or setting should be used. These settings should complement the story, helping to move it forward, and giving the impression that such a place could actually exist. Scene changes must be natural, otherwise the smooth flow of the story will be disrupted, jarring the reader's attention.

Theme

Every story must have a theme, it must say something about life, and have significance to the reader. This does not mean it has to be a penetrating insight, or even a moral, but a statement about the human experience. Theme is the dominant idea you explore in your story. It can be a familiar proverb, a maxim, or a recognisable saying, wise or witty in nature. A theme could be 'going off with strangers may be dangerous', or 'sacrificing everything for the love of a partner'. 'Helping others brings its own rewards'. The story's theme must be highlighted through the actions of the characters.

Viewpoint

Should you write in the third person or first person narrative? Frankly, there are few opportunities in British comics to choose viewpoint: the 'third person' form is preferred, except when it comes to the teenage girl's photo-strip stories. In this case, the 'first person' narrative is the dominant one. The appeal of writing in the first person is that the story is told from the lead character's point of view. The reader becomes a confidant, sharing feelings and thoughts with the character. The drawbacks are that you can only describe what the character telling the story can see, and the character must appear throughout the story.

Credibility

Everything you write must have credibility — it could just possibly happen. All good novels have this about them. A reader will become more engrossed in a story, and eager to find out what is going to happen to the characters, (i.e. buy the next issue!) if the story is *real* to them.

Adult Comics

A word about 'adult' comics and newspaper strips. This may come as a surprise, but the majority of comic collectors (as opposed to the 'general' reader) are adults. Most prefer the American and European comics, with their mature themes and storylines. Sadly, comic strips in Britain are almost solely published for audiences of between under-five, and eleven years of age. There are one or two titles that can be enjoyed by a teenage, and even adult audience, but these are few and far between. Fleetway's flagship sci-fi title, 2000 A.D., has been an overwhelming success, with a wide-ranging audience. Yet it still remains the exception to the rule. One or two independent publishers have tried to publish a regular comic aimed at a more mature readership. These tend to be small print run titles, with a low, perhaps non-existent page rate, and there has yet to be such a title that has stayed the course. This may be because the general public are still unaware that comics are no longer 'kids fodder', but a respected medium in their own right.

Newspaper Strips

Newspaper strips are three-panelled stories that are featured on the comics page of the popular daily newspapers. The number of strips appearing in British papers is diminishing, and unfortunately there isn't much chance of selling anything here. Having said this, a number of magazines are now using this type of strip, and there may be openings, if your work has potential. If you feel you have an idea that is suited to this medium, you will need to find a good artist (unless you happen to be one — and we mean *good*. Mediocre won't cut it) and work up at least twelve sample strips to send to an editor. If your strip is syndicated (i.e. sold to newspapers around the world) it is possible to make a lot of money from this type of work. The drawback is your strip would need to be of the same quality as *Garfield, Andy Capp*, or *Fred Bassett* to sell. Are you really that good?

Here is an example of how a newspaper strip script is laid out, and how the artist-letterer interpreted the stories. . . .

DODO (Newspaper strip)

1. Dodo and Delilah watch Man as he passes by. Man is carrying a spear (a wooden spear with a stone shaft) in his hand, and is walking barefoot. A small rock is directly in his path. Delilah looks disgusted.

DELILAH: UGGH! WHAT IS *THAT*?

2. Head-shot of Dodo and Delilah.

DODO: OH, THAT'S MAN.

3. They watch as Man trips over the rock and falls flat on his face.

TRIP!
MAN: OOF!
DODO: PATHETIC, ISN'T IT?

1. Dodo stands before a half-finished sign. Nailed to a post are three rough pieces of wood. On the first piece of wood is Scrawled the word *BEWARE*. Beneath this, on the second piece of wood, is the word *OF*. Beneath this, a third piece of wood, with the word *FALLING*. Dodo looks puzzled.

2. A giant piano falls out of the sky, squashing Dodo flat.

BLAANNG!

3. A flattened and stunned Dodo staggers past Big Auk. Big Auk carries a hammer, and a fourth piece of rough wood, with the word *PIANOS* scrawled on it.

DODO: DON'T BOTHER ON MY ACCOUNT.

1. Dodo and Delilah are face-to-face in a clearing. Dodo has a wicked smirk on his face as he winks at Delilah.

DODO: HIYA, TOOTS! HOW ABOUT A QUICK ROLL IN THE HAY?

2. Delilah walks away, scornfully. Dodo looks stunned.

DELILAH: NOT JUST NOW, I'VE GOT A HEADACHE!

3. Close-up of Dodo, looking miserable.

DODO: IF THEY ALL CARRY ON LIKE THAT, WE'LL BE EXTINCT BEFORE YOU KNOW IT!

1. Dodo is wearing a large sign around his neck. The sign reads: SAVE THE DODO! Delilah looks at him, puzzled.

DELILAH: WHAT *ARE* YOU DOING?

2. Dodo scowls. Delilah looks surprised.

DODO: GETTING IN PRACTICE!

Of the five main companies, D. C. Thomson are the easiest for the new writer to break into. But these days, a lot of material is produced 'in-house', or are reprints of old stories, so there is not as much work as there used to be. There are always opportunities for good writers at the other companies, apart from TV Times Publications. Look-In is a closed shop for new writers, and many experienced ones for that matter, and is not worth trying. Suron International Publications publishes the British edition of the American satirical magazine, *Mad*. They do buy scripts from British writers, but have special requirements, and it is best to contact the editor with ideas before writing up a full script. Fleetway does use freelance writers, but again, a lot of strips are produced 'in-house', or by regular, established writers. This said, if you have a saleable idea, the editors are not going to send you away. Marvel and London Editions are good companies to work for, if you can prove you have the talent. There is a feeling of being part of a team, rather than 'spare cogs in the machinery'!

Don't forget, comic scripts are also required for Special Editions, Holiday Specials and Annuals, which all the companies are now producing. (Each year, approximately 50 annuals are published, most of which need writers.)

Don't expect to be given a serial to write first time out — you're more likely to be asked to write 'fill-in' scripts until you have proved your worth to an editor. Comic companies are continually on the look out for imaginative writers, but it is hard to make that initial 'first break' unless you are very good. Editors are usually willing to encourage writers who show potential, but at the same time, they must give consideration to their experienced writers, many of whom have been writing for them for years.

You may like to consider joining *The Society Of Strip Illustration* (SSI), an organisation set up in 1977 by a group of professional comic creators. They accept both full and associate members to their ranks. (An associate is a person who is not yet working full-time in comics, but wishes to work in the medium.) The society is open to writers, artists, editors, in fact anyone who is professionally concerned with comics, newspaper strips and strip illustration. This is a good way of meeting other creators, hearing news of new openings in the comic field, and making new friends. The Society publishes a monthly newsletter, and holds monthly meetings and an annual convention in London. Their address is: 7 Dilke Street, Chelsea, London. SW3 4JE.

With the current popularity of comics, there is an influx of new talent trying to break in to the medium. You must be sure you can match the type of stories that are being published now. So, having read this chapter once, go out and buy a pile of comics and then read this chapter again. When you are sure you understand what is required, go and write your comic script. And the best of luck!

Chapter Three

Writing the American Comic Strip

Before we discuss writing techniques, a word must be said about the quality of writing required.

British writers *can* break in to the American market. (In fact, there is a current boom for British writers.) American editors are impressed by the writing and somewhat anarchic approach to storytelling of some British writers. The doors are open across the Atlantic for anyone with talent, but you have to be good — very good.

Basically, there are two ways of writing a comic script for the American comic books. The first is very similar to British scriptwriting; the other is commonly referred to as 'the Marvel Method'. (The name and style originates from the Marvel comic company.).

Whilst many dozens of small, independent, American comic companies exist, the big four must be Marvel Entertainments Group, (better known as Marvel Comics) DC Comics, First Comics and Eclipse Comics. Of these, the last three use a similar format when laying out a comic script. (We will discuss 'the Marvel Method' shortly.) It is worth going through the procedure of writing American comic books step-by-step:

Choose the Company you Wish to Write For

The majority of Marvel and DC's output concentrates on the popular super hero comics. Most people recognise the names of the most famous characters: *Batman, The X-Men, Superman, The Hulk, Wonder Woman, Spider-Man*. But if such names as *The New Mutants, Captain Atom, The Teen Titans, Daredevil, Justice League International* and *X-Factor* mean nothing to you, you should go and buy the latest issues

37

of the American monthly comics. These can be found in most newsagents. Before you start, you need to know what you're writing, and for whom. It must be said that DC and Marvel are the best companies to break into. Between them they publish around 80-100 titles, and together sell in excess of fifteen million copies a month. No other company comes close. Most of the stories written for these companies are by freelance writers. Marvel purchases between 600 and 800 manuscripts a year, and both companies encourage unsolicited synopses, but not full scripts.

First and Eclipse, whose readership tend to be slightly older, do produce super hero comics (though in our opinion, none as good as the two major companies); also science fiction, horror, and detective titles. They publish titles with collections of short stories. Many of these stories only run to eight pages at most. Marvel and DC have also started publishing titles with collections of short stories, based on their super hero characters. (The normal length of a strip is between 22 to 25 pages.) Eclipse have an open-door policy towards new writers who wish to write a script for one of their books. If your script is good, they will seriously consider it.

First and Eclipse work with a small number of new, unpublished writers each year, and Eclipse claim to publish comics for 'the discerning reader'. Unlike Marvel and DC, whose comics may be found in newsagents, Eclipse and First comics are only sold in speciality comic shops in Britain. (The addresses of some of the best are given at the back of this book.)

Eclipse is the only company whose entire run of titles are 'creator-owned'. This means that the copyright to the series remains in the possession of the creators. This does mean that they have little use for the 'fill-in' stories, except for their titles which feature collections of short stories. However, if you can interest them in a series you have created, you have the chance of writing a regular comic book.

Comico The Comic Company, is, as it were, the fifth of the major companies. They are the youngest, and prefer the writer to submit material together with an artist of his choice, although this is not essential. (The other companies will match the writer to the artist, and, in all honesty, this is the safest policy. You may lose the chance of selling your script by submitting work with an artist who is considered unsuitable.)

All companies are interested in finding new talent. After many years in the doldrums, American comics are enjoying a new wave of popularity. It is now 'in' to be seen reading comics, whatever age you are. Doctors, scientists, secretaries, politicians, pop stars and actors read comics. More comics are being published and sold now, and that means more writers are needed. If you can come up with the goods, you'll find yourself being asked for more.

Write and Submit a Synopsis of Your Proposed Story

Choose the series you want to write for, develop a story, write up and send off a synopsis. It should be no longer than two pages, double spaced, with your name and address on each sheet. Don't send any more than two synopses at one time: all the companies receive many dozens of unsolicited synopses every week. They will look at all of them; the majority will be returned as unsuitable. (Remember, always include at least two International Reply Coupons, available from Post Offices, with each submission, if you expect a reply. Also take into account that sea mail takes that much longer to arrive than airmail. It may prove cheaper, but if you are serious about working for the American market, sea mail is not worth the trouble.)

The synopsis should explain what the story is about, what will happen, what you are trying to say, and how the story will climax. You don't need to use dialogue in the synopsis. All that is required is a breakdown of the story. If an editor likes what he sees, he will ask you to write up a plot.

There will always be a problem writing for books with on-going stories. Since your first script, if accepted, will be a 'fill-in', only used when the regular creators miss their deadlines, your story should be self-contained, and not affect the characters of the series in the long term. Also, consider the comic you've chosen to submit a synopsis to. If the book has had the same writer for an extended period, and the writer has never missed a deadline, it is hardly a wise move to offer a story to this comic, since it is unlikely to be used. (A prime example is Marvel's *The X-Men*, which has been written continuously for fourteen years by scriptwriter Chris Claremont.) It is better to choose a comic which changes its writers regularly. Your synopsis will then stand a much greater chance of being looked at.

Write up and Submit a Detailed Plot

This is an expanded synopsis, running to seven or eight double spaced pages in length. It is written in the form of a short story, but generally without the use of dialogue. An example of a page from the plot of our *Tidal Force* series is shown here. The plot tells the actual story, giving full details of events that will transpire, before it is broken down into comic strip form. If the editor likes your plot, you will be two-thirds there, and will be asked to write the comic strip.

TIDAL FORCE 7
"The Diabolical Doctor Decay!"
Synopsis by
Creative Imaginations

We begin with Tidal Force, bursting through the depths of the ocean, cradling the withered, dying form of his girlfriend, Shareen, in his arms. An astonished holidaymaker on board the QE2 cruise ship watches in astonishment as Tidal Force flies into the air. . . .

Deep underground, in the sewers of New York City, we pan around the slime-infested walls, which are lit up by wooden torches. Pulling back, we find ourselves in a clearing, ankle-deep in sludge and waste. There are people down here, human rats. Four are muscle-bound thugs recruited from the alleys of the city, armed with Uzi weapons. They shrink back, trying to hide their fear, in the presence of another man. Doctor Decay. A man disfigured beyond all recognition, his face decaying, crumbling, each time he speaks. There is but one thought on his mind:

"Tidal Force must die."

Decay holds up a newspaper. The headline screams of Decay's defeat at Tidal Force's hands only yesterday (last month to us.) The reporter accuses Decay of being spineless, of running away from the battle.

Write up the Comic Strip

The 'Marvel Method' aside, most American comic scripts are laid out the same way as those aimed at the British market. However, there are a few minor differences to note.

First, always mark clearly, the page of the comic you are writing. This does not automatically mean the page of the script you are on. You will find it sometimes takes more than one page of script to detail what is happening on the page of a comic. So, even though you may be on page six of your script, you may actually only have reached page four of the comic strip itself. Make sure it is clear to an editor what page you are writing. So, for instance, at the top of the sixth page of your script, you may write,
PAGE FOUR
followed by
PANEL 1
and then proceed to give the directions to the artist.

Americans use both captions and Blurbs (or Thoughts, as they are also known), are a form of third-person narrative. They allow the writer to examine or suggest a character's feelings from the character's point of view.

Just to confuse, art directions are written in capitals, while captions, blurbs, and dialogue are written in small characters. Sound effects are denoted by the synonym SFX, and remain in capitals.

The first page of a comic book is called the 'splash' page. This is usually one large panel that starts off the story to best effect, but these are generally only used when writing the full-length (22-25 pages) comic strips.

The majority of American comic strip pages have an average of six panels to a page. You can have more, up to nine panels to a page, but the page will look crowded if you're not careful. You must work out how many panels will be required for each page, and what size they should be. Scenes featuring people talking can be fitted into relatively small panels, while action scenes need larger ones to give the desired effect.

Unlike British comics, each new comic page begins the panel numbering anew: so, for instance, Page Eight may run from panels one through five, Page Nine panels one through seven, Page Ten panels one through six, etc.

Otherwise, the scripts are laid out in exactly the same manner as described in *Writing The British Comic Strip*.

American comics carry a number of 'to be continued . . .' stories. If, by chance, you get the opportunity to write the continuation of a story, it should begin with a short re-cap of the preceding issue, to remind readers what has occurred. The re-caps should be shown within the first four pages of the story, and occupy no more than a page, otherwise you will bore those readers who *did* read the last issue.

The Marvel Method

Basically, what happens, is that the writer comes up with a plot, not a complete script. This is very similar to a story synopsis, but with much more detail. The script of the plot can be as long as the strip itself, twenty pages or more. This is sent to the artist to draw up in pencil. The pencilled artwork is then returned to the writer to write in the copy: narrative, dialogue, etc, onto the actual artwork itself, in pencil. This done, the artwork is sent to the inker to ink. When this has been completed, it will be passed on to the letterer, and finally the colourist.

It seems a convoluted way of working, and it is — but, it works! Marvel comics are the most popular in Britain and America. Their output is phenomenal, and most of their products make a satisfying read.

Not all scriptwriters enjoy working 'the Marvel Method'. Even though the scriptwriter is still required to create the plot and narrative, the responsibility for deciding how panels are laid out on a page, is left to the artist. In Marvel's defence, other writers find this method stimulating. After all, the artist is only as good as the plot he is given. Both the writer and artist can work unrestricted initially and tidy up when they finally collaborate. In essence, it's still your story. The best way to view the situation is that you and the artist are a partnership, each using the knowledge and experience in your respective fields, to create a story.

What is Required of a Writer Working for Marvel?

Again, stage one is to submit the synopsis of a story. This synopsis must be kept short, stating the facts directly. There is no need to go into detail about what will happen in a certain scene — editors are only concerned with finding out if you have a strong story to tell. Your exciting scene descriptions can wait until you are asked to expand the synopsis into a full plot.

The company thrives on the 'super hero' comics: Marvel were the first company to make such comics respectable to more than just children; and this is still the best opportunity for the new writer. (By 'new', we mean experienced comic writers who have not yet worked for American comics — scriptwriters who are still struggling to sell stories to British comics have little hope of making it here.)

If an editor likes the synopsis, he will ask the writer to develop it into a full plot. The plot is a guide to the artist. With Marvel, the writer doesn't tell the artist exactly what to draw. You simply explain what you would like to see happen on a page, but it is left to the artist to decide how many panels are necessary, and how the illustrations will appear in those panels.

How Do You Lay Out a Marvel Plot?

Put your name, the title and issue number of the comic you're writing, (if known), the title of the story and the number of pages the story will run to, at the top of the first page, together with the date you submitted the story. On subsequent pages, put your name, the title of the book and/or story title, and page number. Some writers put their address and 'phone number on the first page as well — there's nothing like playing it safe!

The layout of the plot varies with individual writers. Some make it clear to the artist what they expect to happen on each page of the strip. Others will write a full plot without detailing where each page begins and ends, leaving this up to the artist to decide. Either is acceptable, though to begin with, it's best to stick with the first type of format. You want to be sure the editor understands exactly what is going to happen on each page. (Selling stories is difficult enough without creating additional problems for yourself.)

From then on, it is a reasonably simple job to write up the plot (though it helps to have a good story to begin with!) The first page will be the 'splash page', and usually but not always, the title page. (There have been stories where the title appeared in the middle, or at the end. But for now, keep it simple — you can play clever when you've established yourself as a writer to be reckoned with.)

After that, it is a matter of describing what is going to happen on each page. There is no need to indicate specific lines of dialogue, you'll do this when the pencilled artwork of the story is returned to you. So, taking our own character series, *Tidal Force*, as an example, this is how we would lay out the script of the plot in the Marvel Method — the finished artwork to accompany this plot is reproduced here for you to study.

Page 1: (Splash panel/title page): We open our story with a dramatic shot of Tidal Force bursting up from the depths of the ocean. In his arms, he holds the crumpled, withered body of a woman. It is his girlfriend, Shareen. She is only twenty-five, but now looks like an old woman in her Eighties. TF looks furious — he is in no mood for games. It is a bright, sunny day, with seagulls flying overhead. In the background of the picture is the cruise ship, the QE2.

Page 2: On the deck of the boat are holiday-makers, dressed in short-sleeved shirts, bikinis, etc. A man is looking through a pair of binoculars at the sight of Tidal Force leaping out of the sea. He splutters incoherently at his wife, sitting in a

deckchair, to come see the flying man. She ignores him, deciding he's 'off the bottle' from now on.

Cut to New York City: then deep underground, in the sewers, (make it interesting — slime dripping off the walls, rats scurrying about; a home from home!). An area of the sewer is lit with wooden torches fitted to the walls. Surrounding Doctor Decay are four muscle-bound thugs, all armed with 'Uzi' sub-machine guns. Doc is raging about an article in a newspaper, which calls him a coward for running from his battle with Tidal Force. Tearing off one of his gloves, he touches the newspaper with his gnarled, blotted and discoloured hand. The newspaper disintegrates. This, swears Doc, is what will happen to Tidal Force when next they meet!

You continue to write in this way until you come to the end of the story. When it's completed, off it goes to the editor, who, with luck, will be pleased with your script. He will then choose an artist to illustrate your story.

A few words about the artist's job are in order here. As we've explained, the artist takes the plot as a guide to what he will draw, and decides what will appear in each panel. You could liken the artist's job to that of a director of a silent movie. He must tell a visual story without sound. It's the artist, too, who paces the script, making it run smoothly, from beginning to end. Marvel artists are the real storytellers, without the use of words.

When the pencilled artwork has been completed, it's sent to the writer for scripting the copy: dialogue, captions, sound effects, etc.

Here is an example of how dialogue is laid out in the Marvel Method.

Page 7
1. Dr Decay: This city is mine!
2. Dr Decay: My powers protect me from permanent injury! It's unfortunate that you're not so lucky!
3. CAP: Tidal Force drew upon the moisture of the air to increase his strength!
4. TF: Your evil has destroyed the lives of hundreds of innocent people! Now feel *my* power!
5. Dr Decay: *YAAAAGGH!*
6. TF: You're *sick* — crazed! But this time you've gone *too far!* I'm going to stop you — once and for all!

It is your job to bring the pictures alive, to flesh out the characters, building up the tension and drama towards the inevitable climax. Through the words you write, the reader must be swept along, unable to resist turning the page to see what happens next. You must give the reader all the essential information, whilst developing the natural theme of the story. Your dialogue must sound natural, and in keeping with the individual characters.

In effect, you are writing a comic script as you would for other companies, but instead of indicating the art directions, you only write for the copy in each panel.

An interesting aspect of this job, is that you must indicate where the words are to be *placed* in each panel. You do this by numbering each part of the copy on the actual script, and then marking these same numbers, in pencil, on the artwork, where you want the letterer to put the captions, dialogue balloons, sound effects, etc. People are used to reading from left to right, so it is important to arrange the balloons in the correct order of importance, so the reader, at a glance, will know who is speaking first. The artist has to be aware of this so as not to create any awkwardness when placing the characters in the panels. Spiked balloons should be used if you want a special 'shock' effect.

If we take the first two pages of the plot of *TIDAL*

FORCE: "The Diabolical Doctor Decay" as an example, it should look something like this:

PAGE 1
  1. CAP: Ten miles out from the Florida Coast. . . .
  2. Tidal Force: Doctor Decay! You're going to PAY for this!

PAGE 2
  1. CAP: On the deck of the QE2 . . .
  2. MAN: Holey Moley! Myra! Come and look at this! It's a flying man!
  3. Wife: Herman, sit down! You're making a spectacle of yourself! It's only a dolphin! Or a poy-pose! Lotsa poy-puses out here!
  4. Wife (T): No more'a the HARD stuff for him 'til we get home!
  5. CAP: New York City, three hours later. . . .
  6. CAP: The sewers of New York are infested with rats. Not all are of the four-legged variety. . . .
  7. Thug 1:   C'mon, Doc! Calm down! Tension ain't good fer a person! You'll burst summat!
  8. Thug 2:   Yeah! We know you ain't no coward! No matter what the papers say! Who cares what they print?
  9. Decay: I care! These fools believe I ran from my fight with that muscle-bound oaf, Tidal Force! They jeer at me! Laugh at me!
 10. Decay: Well, no more! The next time we meet, Tidal Force will suffer the same fate as this pile of journalistic codswallop! He will DIE — at my hands!

There's More!

A few additional tips when writing up the script:

* When you want to emphasise certain words, either underline them, or mark them in capitals in the script.

* If you want a word, or sentence to appear in italics, indicate this on the script too.
* If the character in question is thinking, indicate so with a capital T in brackets (T).

Creators receive credits on all their stories. As we have said, all companies are on the lookout for talented script-writers who can meet their needs and deadlines. Recently, comic companies have been publishing weekly and fort-nightly comic books, with four or five eight-page series to each book. Whether or not these will prove popular with an American audience remains to be seen. If these titles continue to flourish, with more weekly titles being published, there will be even more demand for new writers like you!

Marvel, like all American comic companies, treat their creators very well. (This wasn't always the case — in the past, American creators received the same treatment as British ones — so there's still hope on this side of the water!)

Compared to British comics, American comic books pay well — very well, for the top scriptwriters and artists. They pay the normal flat fee for a comic book script. For the beginner, this is approximately $1000 for a 22-page comic book, with a royalty on top of this, after a certain number of copies of a comic have been sold. The best American comic sells over 600,000 copies a month. When you consider that the majority of the top writers churn out four or five comic books each and every month, that soon amounts to a great deal of money! (Marvel claim that their top writers make over $300,000 a year.) Most companies pay on acceptance, though First sometimes pays on publication) with Comico claiming to pay 5 days after acceptance — better than any British company.

There is now a system which allows you to keep copyright on a character or series that you create. These are known as 'creator-owned', as opposed to those owned by the company. This does not apply to all characters; most would not sell in large enough quantities for it to be worth bothering about. However, if you come up with a series and characters that you believe have potential, American comic companies give you an opportunity unheard of in Britain, to discuss the matter, and come to an agreement in everyone's best interest.

It is worth remembering that spelling is different for the US market — 'Color' rather than 'colour', 'tire', not 'tyre', 'center' for 'centre', etc. Editors will correct any spelling mistakes you might make, but they will be more impressed by a writer who has done his homework, and has saved them valuable time. American terms should also be used. They travel in 'elevators', not 'lifts', and babies wear 'diapers', not 'nappies'. There are dozens of other American terms that can be used. Buy an American dictionary and add it to your reference library.

We hope this chapter has been of some use to you, and that you will try writing for American comics some day. You have nothing to lose, and a great deal to gain. For those who make it, the rewards are plentiful.

Chapter Four

Writing the Licensed Series

The licensed character series — characters based on toys, films or television series' — is an expanding market.

There are hundreds of licensed character series, including *The Care Bears, Ghostbusters, Sindy, The Get Along Gang, The Masters Of The Universe, Acorn Green, The Ewoks, Spider-Man, Thomas The Tank Engine, She-Ra, Lasertag Academy, Winnie-The-Pooh, Defenders of the Earth, The Muppet Babies, The Nosy Bears, Thundercats, My Little Pony, American Tail, Captain Power, Inspector Gadget*, plus Disney and Hanna-Barbera characters, and many others.

This is a closed market for many writers. Why? Simply because they don't make an effort to research and understand the characters they are writing about.

There have always been books and comics based on popular film and television series. *The Professionals, Dr. Who, The Man From U.N.C.L.E., Bugs Bunny, Thunderbirds, Lost In Space, Kung Fu, Planet Of The Apes*. These, and hundreds more, have been immortalised in comic strips and text stories. Copies have sold in tens of thousands to eager fans, who will buy anything based on their favourite programmes.

It's only in the past eight years that the licensed character series has exploded into a multi-million dollar industry. It started with toy manufacturers who came up with a new product — the 'collectable' series. They began to flood the market with toy series' that featured more than one character. (In the case of the Care Bears, and Care Bear Cousins, there are over twenty characters to the series!) Nowadays, a toy will have the backing of a TV series (usually animated), a series of books, and possibly even its own comic. Toy manufacturers invest millions of dollars a year to advertise a new product, from laser guns to ponies with rainbow-coloured flowing manes.

It is worth considering that, whilst licensed toy series are created for children, they are also developed to appeal to adults too. (There's a bit of the child in all of us!) This is especially true of the plush toys, such as The Nosy Bears, The Get Along Gang and The Popples. Adults will buy these toys as amusing or sentimental presents for their partners.

After a series has been created the toy manufacturer will contact television, book and comic companies to see if they would be interested in buying the license for their toys. When contracts have been signed, the TV and publishing companies must find someone to write stories based on the toy characters. This is where we come in!

It should be noted that manufacturers do not expect a toy series to last for more than three years. Those that do, (and The Care Bears and The Transformers are prime examples) are considered to have risen beyond a limited series and may receive cult status as toys, in the manner of marbles and roller skates. But whilst the toy series is on the market, there are intense marketing factors at work.

Every book, comic and television show based on a licensed series, has to be written by someone. So why not you?

Firstly, you must ask yourself, do you want to write a story based on a licensed toy or television series? We know many writers who pale at the thought of trying to write a children's story with a beginning, middle and end, which may be as short as 350 words. (The most we've written for a story based on a licensed character is 3000 words.) You may feel that writing a 350 word story is the easiest job in the world! But as a test, go away now and write a story which features a plot, a resolution and an understanding of the characters (which may be as many as eight in one story) in just 500 words. It may come as some surprise to find out how difficult it really is. Writers who can do this, and do it well, are in short supply.

Editors are crying out for writers who can produce top quality scripts to tight deadlines. If you are such a person, you are on the way to making a tidy sum of money on a regular basis. (Once you are established, editors will come back to you for more work. They have no wish to lose someone of your calibre to another company.)

Some people are embarrassed by what they are asked to write.

To take an example of a popular licensed series, if asked to write a story based on the Care Bears, you would be required to use the type of speech that the Bears use amongst themselves. If the thought of writing stories featuring such phrases as "fuzzy" and "snuggly" makes you want to bring up lunch, then go find another market, 'cos this one ain't for you.

Now that we've disposed of nine-tenths of our audience we'll continue . . . The actual mechanics of writing for the licensed series is quite simple: Research! Research! Research! This part of the process cannot be emphasised strongly enough. Without research you cannot begin to know what the series is about. Therefore, you cannot write a story. Research does not have to be a chore — with licensed characters it's usually interesting, and fun!

There are two ways to research a series. When an editor contacts us to write a new licensed series that has not yet been released on the market we ask for the 'bible' for the series. This 'bible' contains full background information on the series. If it is a good 'bible' it will also contain in-depth character profiles (on how each character acts, reacts, thinks, and speaks and any other information that may help the writer). Locations will be described in detail, (such as Snake Mountain — Skeletor's hideout in *The Masters Of The Universe* — or Care-a-Lot, home of the *Care Bears*) and accessories (clothes, weapons, etc.). 'Bibles' are a godsend to a deadline-pressed writer.

The second way to research is to investigate whether anything has already been produced on the series. There will usually be books, videos and perhaps comics available. We don't mind spending out on a set of comics or books, or even a video, because we know our investment will easily be returned. We also video tape any television programmes that are being broadcast on the series at the time.

We then spend hours studying the information we have collected, immersing ourselves in the series and the characters, until we're sure we fully understand what is required. Even then we haven't finished. Before writing a word of a story we make numerous sets of notes about the series and characters for our own benefit which we keep on file, each series in a separate file. Only after all this preparation do we sit down in front of our word processors and begin to plot and write the stories.

You may think that we're exaggerating what is expected of writers. But consider this — how can you possibly understand the characters and their motives unless you are first willing to research their backgrounds? This pays dividends. An editor recently confided that we are the first writers she turns to when she needs stories for a licensed series. Why? Because we instinctively understand what writing for a licensed series is about, and what she will need in terms of a story. We did not appear on the writing scene with all this knowledge tucked away inside our heads. We had to learn the ways of writing for this market from the ground floor. If we can succeed, so can you.

A question all writers are asked is: where do the ideas come from? In one respect, the writer of the licensed series has an advantage over his colleagues. The hard work of creating the series has already been done for us. Each piece of information that has been gathered is a potential plot. This is where research repays the writer. If you've done your homework properly the ideas should be flooding your mind, and you will be scribbling furiously away before the Muse gets up and leaves. Your stories will come from your characters, from their backgrounds, from where they live and what they eat. You will get ideas from throwaway lines in the 'bibles' and what at first seemed totally useless information, featured in the television shows. More ideas will come from watching children playing with their toys, (especially if the toys are from the series you are writing about) and from talking to them about what they enjoy reading in stories. (This helps if you have a natural empathy with children. We love 'em. Hey, without them, we would be out of a job!)

An important aspect of working on the licensed series is the writing itself. For a start, it's sensible to throw away that Writer's Training Manual you're always referring to whenever you start a story. In writing the licensed series — and remember it will be marketed at children — purple prose *is* allowed, just so long as you don't overdo it. In fact, it can be fun. You can also go wild with exclamation marks, especially in the dialogue.

Dialogue

Dialogue is an important matter to consider. Editors have to return a lot of stories because the dialogue is poorly written. If you have researched properly, you should already know how each character speaks. The baddies usually cackle a lot and make threats they can't keep, while the good guys (and girls) have a pure, noble spirit which comes through in their dialogue. Each character is different. It is no good applying dialogue based on one character for all the characters you write.

Characterisation

A major failing of new writers to this market is in characterisation. Again, we come back to that old failsafe — research! You must research the characters before you attempt to write about them. If you have a character doing something in your story which goes against all his past history, your script had better have a twist to explain this peculiar state of affairs, or you won't sell the story.

Another failing is the lack of characterisation. With all the information at hand, there should be no problems in writing fully-developed characters unless you haven't bothered to research the series first. Remember, the interest a reader has depends almost entirely upon the characters. (This may come as a disappointment, but children who buy books and comics based on the licensed series are not interested in styles of writing. They don't buy these publications to read the works of 'Joe Bloggs — writer'. They buy them because they feature their favourite toy, film or television characters.) That is not to say that your writing has no worth, or that you can write any old rubbish. Children are more intelligent than most adults! They will soon find better ways to spend their money if a comic or book is poorly written, or produced.

In the licensed character series, you only have space enough for those characteristics that are relevant; but you must bring the characters to life. Even though they are only toys they must move and speak like real people. It's vital to ensure that they don't fade into the background.

The licensed series should contain the same ingredients as any other type of story: a good, strong plot, conflict, exciting action scenes, a smooth, steady pace, believability, a powerful visual content, and well-defined characters. (See *Writing The British Comic Strip*). If you mix all these together, you have the recipe of successful story writing.

All right, let's assume that after reading this you've decided to write a story for a licensed series (and if it is after reading this then where's our 10%?). What markets can you realistically be asked to write for? Well, there are three major markets in Britain. Comics, books, and cassette-books.

Comics

In Britain, the majority of comics now being published are based on toy and TV series. (They are produced by a number of different companies, the most respected being Marvel Comics.) This is because British comics are still mainly published for young children, with very few titles being marketed for the 11+ age group. And it's the young children to whom the toy manufacturers are aiming their product. If you want to write comic strips, look over what is currently being published. If anything appeals to you, write up a synopsis and send it to the editor concerned. (See *Writing The British Comic Strip*)

In America, even today, there are very few comic books based on licensed series. As far as we know, they are all published by Marvel Comics. If you want to write comic strips based on a licensed series for the States, check out what Marvel are currently producing. You'll find copies of the latest issues in most comic shops, (those shops specialising in selling only comics) or comic dealers. See the Appendix at the back of this book for more information. As usual for the States, write up a synopsis, and send it to one of the editors concerned. (See our chapter on *Writing The American Comic Strip*)

Books

Books are a good market, if you can get in. The Catch-22, of course, being that, if you haven't written anything based on licensed characters before, publishers aren't interested. However, if you have written children's stories that have been published, or can show that your writing abilities are suitable for the needs of a given publisher, then you may still have a good chance of being offered work. Once you have your first licensed series story under your belt, more will follow.

Cassette-Books

The third market is for cassette-books (occasionally referred to as audio-books.) These are books that come accompanied with a cassette upon which is an audio version of the story for children to listen to. For more information on how to write for this market, read *Writing Cassette-Books*.

Payment

Payment for a story based on a licensed series will always be a flat fee, with no royalties offered. Unlike creating original comic strip series, this is understandable, considering that the copyright to the series' remains with the toy manufacturers. However, depending upon the company you write for, payment can be quite lucrative. Thankfully, the majority of publishers treat their freelancers well.

Deadlines

The single word that causes many a great writer to break out in cold sweats is deadlines. We all have them. We all moan about them. We all have to meet them. A writer of the licensed character series' has to face tougher deadlines than anyone else in the profession. There have been times when we have received a 'phone call in an afternoon from an editor needing 'a set of stories, by tomorrow morning'. Once a publisher asked for four 1000 word books, based on the girls' doll, Sindy, in three days. Thanks to access to a 'fax' machine we delivered word-perfect copy on time, but it did mean cancelling any plans we had for the evenings, and working around the clock. (Sleep and food? — ah, yes, we remembered that, just!!)

We happen to enjoy this sort of quirky, disruptive life, where we're never quite sure what is going to land in our laps, but we do understand, and sympathise, with those writers who prefer regular hours of working. This must be your decision. You may never be faced with such short deadlines, but if you are and you refuse, you may not be asked again. (Of course, you can charge more when deadlines are close — you're not a doormat for publishers to trample over.) Most publishers respect the writer who can work to short deadlines. If you are such a person, you may find yourself being used more often.

Speaking from personal experience, there may come a time when you are asked to write a story based on a licensed series for a comic or book publisher, but when it is completed, you find the proposed book or comic has been shelved. Sadly, there is not much you can do about it. You will not receive a 'kill-fee' for the work you've done, and if you complain too loudly, you will only discourage an editor from using you again. In these cases, you can do little but grumble under your breath, and then start on another story.

However, signalling your displeasure in a gentle, diplomatic manner pays dividends, and usually makes an editor think twice before wasting your time again. The meek will never inherit the earth — they'll be too busy writing unwanted comic scripts!

Writing the children's licensed series is for the young-at-heart. If you have the ability to regress back to childhood at an editor's beck and call, you should be writing for this market. It's a fun — and profitable — way to earn a living. It is also satisfying to know that something that you have written is bringing pleasure to hundreds of thousands of children.

After all, where else can you get paid for watching cartoons and reading comics? We wouldn't want to do anything else!

Finally, here's an example of a comic strip for very young children. There are no speech balloons, just text underneath the pictures. There is a market for such work, and many magazines rely on it. It can be seen in Marvel's "Thomas The Tank Engine".

THE GORILLA FAMILY SCRIPT

7. Little Rodney Gorilla picked up his bucket and spade. "I'm going to build a sandcastle!" he giggled.

ART: Rodney gorilla is sitting on the beach with a bucket and spade. It's a sunny day, and he's near the sea shore.

Little Rodney Gorilla picked up his bucket and spade. "I'm going to build a sandcastle!" he giggled.

Rodney dug a big hole in the soft sand. Each time he dug, he showered Jogalong Gorilla, who was sunbathing close by. "Do you mind?" she spluttered. "I don't want to be turned into a sandcastle!"

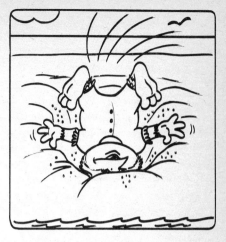

hen Rodney had finished, he ran to
his Mummy for an ice cream. All the
gging had made him very hot. While he
s away, Frumps Gorilla came along.

She tripped over Jogalong, who was busy
trying to clean the sand out of her fur,
and fell into the hole. "Oh furballs!" she
snorted. "What a stupid place to leave a
hole!"

ddenly Frumps noticed that her feet
ere getting wet. "Great galloping
orillas!" she gasped. "The tide's coming
!"

Jogalong heard her sister's cry. "Don't
worry, I'll save you!" she called, running
across the beach towards the lifeguard,
as fast as her legs would carry her.

8. Rodney dug a big hole in the soft sand. Each time he dug, he showered Jogalong Gorilla, who was sunbathing close by. "Do you mind?" she spluttered. "I don't want to be turned into a sandcastle!"

ART: Rodney is deep in a hole in the sand. Jogalong, his sister, is lying on a beach towel. She is covered in sand. In addition, a spade-full of sand is flying through the air towards her.

9. When Rodney had finished, he ran to ask his Mummy for an ice cream. All the digging had made him very hot. While he was away, Frumps Gorilla came along.

ART: Frumps is walking along the beach, reading a comic. She looks just like the other gorillas, but she's wearing a very frumpy, old-fashioned, bathing costume.

10. She tripped over Jogalong, who was busy trying to clean the sand out of her fur, and fell into the hole. "Oh furballs!" she snorted. "What a stupid place to leave a hole!"

ART: Frumps is standing on her head in the hole.

11. Suddenly Frumps noticed that her feet were getting wet. "Great galloping gorillas!" she gasped. "The tide's coming in!"

ART: Picture Frumps struggling to get out of the deep hole. There's water up to her waist already, and more waves are splashing in. From her point of view please — a low angle with the waves above her.

12. Jogalong heard her sister's cry. "Don't worry, I'll save you!" she called, running across the beach towards the lifeguard, as fast as her legs would carry her.

ART: Jogalong is rushing across the sand towards the lifeguard station which is in the distance. She looks worried.

62

Chapter Five

Writing Cassette/Books

In recent years, bookshops, supermarkets and other associated sales outlets have been bombarded with racks full of cassettes and books, sold together wrapped in clear plastic packs. It's the first time that literature has been offered for sale as a true impulse buy. It's an expanding market, and one which is well worth exploring.

The cassette/book concept is simple — a tape containing an exciting children's audio play, married up with a book of the script from which the play was produced. The characters used are normally famous ones from television shows, Disney and suchlike. The idea is that the child listens to the tape whilst following the text in the accompanying book. Throughout the recording, there are special tones recorded to indicate the turn of each page. These prompts make it very easy for a child to follow the action with a combination of ears and eyes, making the package both entertaining and educational. The market share for these products is growing steadily, with more and more companies jumping on the bandwagon. It's not just the independents either — large publishing groups are beginning to devote a department to cassette/books — and many of them need well-written scripts!

Writing for this market is easy once you understand a few simple rules. Grasping several points will mean the difference between success and failure in cassette/book authorship. Most of the companies we deal with complain that a large percentage of the speculative scripts that arrive are constructed without format. However good a story may be, the company simply hasn't got time to devote to hours of editing. The biggest fault lies in the fact that novices write their scripts as if they're going to exist in book form only.

Most publishing companies require all references to

characters in the form of "he said," "she said," "he replied hastily," "they shouted," etc. to be absent. That's the most important point — if you've written the script properly then they're just not necessary. There are two ways to convey who is speaking, and maintain clarity in dialogue. They are your golden rules:

* Introduce your character into the story before they are required to speak any dialogue. This will indicate to the listener/reader who is speaking, without resorting to "he said": E.G.: Terry walked into the sitting room and sat down. "What's for tea?"
* At the end of a line of dialogue, tag on the person's name that it is directed at. E.G.: Terry walked into the sitting room and sat down. "What's for tea, Mum?"

You must avoid confusing the listener/reader — and most scripts of this nature are a compromise in some ways. Often the child will want to read the book without playing the cassette — it must still make sense, and employ correct English throughout. The best way to check if the script is likely to work, is to record it onto a cassette tape yourself, then scrutinise a playback. This will always show up any obvious flaws.

The most effective way of illustrating clearly the difference between a text story and the required cassette/book script, is to see the same story written in each format. The following original Creative Imaginations story is provided, first in conventional book-type text format, and then re-arranged to suit the cassette/book market. At first you may not notice the differences — some are very subtle — but many changes have been made to the cassette/book version. Examine both scripts very carefully, and take note of each alteration.

After you finish reading this chapter, try some cassette/book script alterations for yourself. Find any children's story book, (preferably one of ours!) and alter each story ready for cassette/book recording — it's the best possible practice for you!

BOOK VERSION
THE SECRETS OF CLEMATIS COTTAGE

The old cottage had stood empty for a long time, but today it hummed with life. A new family were moving in. The big white clematis flowers that grew around the door had bloomed as if to welcome the new owners.

"When are the carpets arriving, Mum?" shouted a little girl's voice excitedly.

"Soon Amy, soon!" replied a jolly red-faced woman for what seemed like the hundredth time that morning. "Go and help Adam and your Dad clean out the cupboards!"

Mr and Mrs Berry, together with their two children, Adam and Amy, were the new owners, and today they were moving in. Everyone was excitedly awaiting the arrival of the big removal van full of the family's furniture. Everyone that was, except for a very grumpy bat!

"Huh! This looks like the end of my peace and quiet!" he grumbled, climbing down from an old oak beam in the dark loft. "I wonder what the others think of all this commotion?" He squeezed his way out through a gap in the warm thatch, and screwing his eyes up against the bright sunlight, made his way to the old dovecot above the garage.

The Berry family had bought more than they bargained for. Clematis Cottage had not been completely empty over the last few months. It had a secret — eight of them in fact! A happy gang of animal friends who were guardians of the house.

"Coo, Hello Basil!" smiled Luvva Dove as the short-sighted bat crash-landed in her dovecot. "Awake at last? My oh my, you flew here fast!"

"I haven't got much choice with this row going on!" he snorted, his keen ears twitching as he heard the furniture van approaching.

Luvva Dove giggled and swooped out of the dovecot. "Coo, coo! — must hurry and tell our friends, this is going to be one of our most exciting weekends!" With that she disappeared in the direction of the rhododendron bushes.

The carpet fitters had arrived too, and a man was already hard at work in the study upstairs. "I don't know why they want to keep these old books," he said, carefully moving aside some dusty old encyclopaedias.

"Well I like that!" hissed Sherlock Spider under his breath. He adjusted his magnifying glass to get a better look at the carpet fitter. "I bet he wouldn't be too pleased if someone said that about his house!"

Sherlock was the brains of the secret gang. He was very smart, and his friends always came to him when there was a crisis. It was easy to come up with an answer if you lived in an encyclopaedia.

The carpet fitter's mumbling faded into the distance as he began work on another room. Suddenly a familiar pair of twitching whiskers appeared from a hole in the skirting board, and Marsha Mouse scampered into the study. She sneezed as the thick pile of the new carpet tickled her nose. "This is going to take some getting used to!"

"Begorra! The sky's fallen! Help, help!" a muffled voice reached her ears. Sherlock had heard it too, and crawled out to meet Marsha on the prickly carpet.

"Aha, I deduce that it's O'Blarney, our daft beetle friend!" he cried in alarm. "He must be trapped under this silly carpet."

"Waggling whiskers, what can we do?" gulped Marsha, her eyes widening. "He'll suffocate!"

Meanwhile, out in the garden, Luvva Dove was having an interesting conversation with Flibber the French frog, and Harvey Hedgehog, the remaining two members of the gang. They were sunning themselves in their favourite spot, in the shade of the rhododendron bush. When suddenly . . .

"It's gone, my wedding ring!" Mrs Berry burst into the garden in a terrible state.

"It can't be far, love!" said Mr Berry, trying to console her. "We'll look again, It must be around here somewhere!"

Luvva Dove overheard. "Coo! I'm not so sure!" she said to her friends. "With all this upheaval going on, it could be in the kitchen or behind the cupboard door!"

"Ah, monsieurs, what about inside le van?" said Flibber. "It could have fallen off when she was helping le men move in le furniture!"

"Oh dear! Oh dear!" cried Harvey anxiously, curling up into a prickly ball, "listen!" The deep rumbling roar of the removal van could be heard in the distance.

"Oh la la!, zey have gone!" said Flibber. "There's nothing we can do now my friends!"

"Don't give up, leave it to me! I'll find the ring and be home for tea!" replied Luvva Dove, flying off as fast as her wings would carry her.

Luckily there was a lot of traffic around, and the van was soon stuck in a queue. "Coo, that was a stroke of luck!" she gasped, catching up with the van and landing on top to get her breath back. "I've caught up with the truck!" After a few moments, she scrambled in through the half-open tailgate and began a careful search.

Back in the house, O'Blarney's cries were getting weaker all the time. Sherlock Spider thought fast and scuttled into the next room. He returned puffing and panting a few moments later. "I must take more exercise!" he spluttered.

"Have you got a plan?" squeaked Marsha urgently, looking desperately worried.

"It's elementary my dear Marsha!" said Sherlock grandly. "There's a piece of rotten floorboard just inside the door. If you gnaw through it, I think we can reach him. But hurry, there's no time to lose!"

Marsha didn't need a second telling, and in no time was working away at the soft wood with her sharp teeth. Suddenly another sawing sound reached her ears. She looked up to see Buzzer Bee hovering over her.

"Having troublezzzz?" he asked cheerfully.

"Big trouble!" replied Sherlock Spider, scampering across the room to join his friends. "Buzzer, can you get through that hole?" he said pointing to splintered wood.

"I reckon zzo, but why?"

"O'Blarney's trapped under the carpet. We've got to get him out before he suffocates! You could airlift him to safety!"

Buzzer squeezed through the tiny hole. "I'm on my wayzzz!" Marsha and Sherlock peered into the darkness as the buzzing faded into the distance.

Luvva Dove had found the ring under some dust sheets inside the removal van. At that very moment, she was dashing back with it held safely in her beak.

"You found it!" cried Harvey Hedgehog, uncurling himself

as Luvva Dove landed in the rhododendron bush again.

"Tres bien, but what now my friends?" croaked Flibber Frog.

"Coo, coo. You mustn't look glum! It's up to Harvey now, our prickly pal chum!"

"Gulp! m-me?" wailed Harvey, curling up into a ball again. "N-No f-fear! I might get trampled on or s-something!"

Luvva Dove cooed around her friend. "Coo, come on now Harvey, you must be away! It's up to you to save the day!"

"Oh prickles!" moaned Harvey, popping his nose out to look at Luvva Dove. As nervous as he was, he would do anything for his friends. "I suppose I'll do it for you, but if I get caught I'll be in a jolly bad mood!" With that, he scuttled off across the lawn.

"Madame Dove!" frowned Flibber. "Why send le hedge-hog? I could 'ave done le job instead!"

"Coo, coo, how true!" agreed Luvva Dove. "But to make Harvey brave is something we must do!"

Harvey rushed to the old ivy-covered porch at the back of the cottage. He quickly dropped the ring, then he gave a squeal of fright. He could hear footsteps approaching. "Ooh, ooh. I must curl up!" he cried. Then he thought again "Ohh, oh! No! If they find me, they might use me as a football!"

Back upstairs, it seemed like hours before they heard Buzzer Bee returning. He struggled out of the hole with O'Blarney Beetle hanging lifeless in his thin, black, hairy arms.

"I guezzz I was too late," he mumbled.

"Oh no!" sniffed Marsha.

Sherlock rushed up to the beetle and peered closely at him through his magnifying glass.

"The window!" he cried. "Get him to the window!" Marsha curled her long tail around him, sped up the curtain and out across the window sill.

"Begorra!" mumbled O'Blarney between taking great gulpfuls of the cool air. "That was a bumpy ride!"

The others breathed a sigh of relief, life just wouldn't be the same without their silly beetle friend.

Adam wandered out of the house, staring gloomily at the floor. His face lit up as he caught sight of the ring.

"Hurray!" he burst out, snatching it up. "I've found it!"

"You know, I'd swear that ring wasn't there earlier!" said Mrs Berry, as the family sat down to dinner later that evening.

"Perhaps the fairies brought it!" joked Mr Berry. Adam and Amy burst out laughing.

"Fairies indeed! Next you'll be telling us that animals can talk!"

Basil grumbled to himself. "Hmmph! Little do they know," he sighed, hanging from his favourite perch upside-down in the loft. "This house used to be nice and peaceful until they arrived!"

"Oh, I don't know," smiled Marsha Mouse. "Life can get boring if things are too quiet. Now that we have a new family to look after, I think we'll all be in for a lot of fun!"

CASSETTE/BOOK VERSION

THE SECRETS OF CLEMATIS COTTAGE

The old cottage had stood empty for a long time, but today it hummed with life. A new family were moving in. The big white clematis flowers that grew around the door had bloomed as if to welcome the new owners.

"When are the carpets arriving, Mum?"

"How many more times, Amy. Soon!. "Go and help Adam and your Dad clean out the cupboards!"

Mr and Mrs Berry, together with their two children, Adam and Amy, were the new owners, and today they were moving in. Everyone was excitedly awaiting the arrival of the big removal van full of the family's furniture. Everyone that was, except for a very grumpy bat!

"Huh! This looks like the end of my peace and quiet!" He climbed down from an old oak beam in the dark loft. "I wonder what the others think of all this commotion?" He squeezed his way out through a gap in the warm thatch, and screwing his eyes up against the bright sunlight, made his way to the old dovecot above the garage to see Luvva Dove, his poetic flying friend.

The Berry family had bought more than they bargained for. Clematis Cottage had not been completely empty over the last few months. It had a secret — eight of them in fact!

A happy gang of animal friends who were guardians of the house.

Basil Bat crash-landed in the dovecot. Luvva Dove smiled. "Awake at last? My oh my, you flew here fast!"

"I haven't got much choice with this row going on!" Basil's keen ears twitched as he heard the furniture van approaching.

Luvva Dove giggled and swooped out of the dovecot. "Coo, coo! — must hurry and tell our friends, this is going to be one of our most exciting weekends!" With that she disappeared in the direction of the rhododendron bushes.

The carpet fitters had arrived too, and a man was already hard at work in the study upstairs. He moved some dusty encyclopaedias. "I don't know why they want to keep these old books."

Sherlock Spider was most most annoyed. "Well I like that!" He adjusted his magnifying glass to get a better look at the carpet fitter. "I bet he wouldn't be too pleased if someone said that about his house!"

Sherlock was the brains of the secret gang. He was very smart, and his friends always came to him when there was a crisis. It was easy to come up with an answer if you lived in an encyclopaedia.

The carpet fitter's mumbling faded into the distance as he began work on another room. Suddenly a familiar pair of twitching whiskers appeared from a hole in the skirting board, and Marsha Mouse scampered into the study. She sneezed as the thick pile of the new carpet tickled her nose. "This is going to take some getting used to!" With that, she went in search of Sherlock Spider.

"Begorra! The sky's fallen! Help, help!"

"Aha, Marsha, I deduce that's O'Blarney, our daft beetle friend! He must be trapped under this silly carpet."

"Waggling whiskers, what can we do, Sherlock? He'll suffocate!"

Meanwhile, out in the garden, Luvva Dove was having an interesting conversation with Flibber the French frog, and Harvey Hedgehog, the remaining two members of the gang. They were sunning themselves in their favourite spot, in the shade of the rhododendron bush. When suddenly . . .

"It's gone, my wedding ring!" Mrs Berry burst into the garden in a terrible state.

Mr Berry tried to console his wife. "It can't be far, love! We'll look again, it must be around here somewhere!"

Luvva Dove overheard. "Coo! I'm not so sure! With all this upheaval going on, it could be in the kitchen or behind the cupboard door!"

But Flibber Frog had other ideas — "Ah, monsieurs! What about inside le van? It could have fallen off when she was helping le men move in le furniture!"

Harvey Hedgehog looked worried, and curled himself up into a prickly ball. "Oh dear! Oh dear! listen!" The deep rumbling roar of the removal van could be heard in the distance.

Flibber Frog looked glum. "Oh la la!, zey have gone! There's nothing we can do now my friends!"

But Luvva Dove had other ideas. "Don't give up, leave it to me! I'll find the ring and be home for tea!" She flew off as fast as her wings would carry her.

Luckily there was a lot of traffic around, and the van was soon stuck in a queue. "Coo, that was a stroke of luck! I've caught up with the truck!" After a few moments, she scrambled in through the half-open tailgate and began a careful search.

Back in the house, O'Blarney's cries were getting weaker all the time. Sherlock Spider thought fast and scuttled into the next room. He returned puffing and panting a few moments later. "I must take more exercise!"

Marsha was getting desperate. "Have you got a plan, Sherlock?"

"It's elementary my dear Marsha! There's a piece of rotten floorboard just inside the door. If you gnaw through it, I think we can reach him. But hurry, there's no time to lose!"

Marsha didn't need a second telling, and in no time was working away at the soft wood with her sharp teeth. Suddenly another sawing sound reached her ears. She looked up to see Buzzer Bee hovering over her.

"Having troublezzzz?"

Sherlock Spider scampered across the room to join his friends. "Big trouble, Buzzer! Can you get through that hole?" he said pointing to splintered wood.

"I reckon zzzo, but why?"

"O'Blarney's trapped under the carpet. We've got to get

him out before he suffocates! You could airlift him to safety!"

Buzzer squeezed through the tiny hole. "I'm on my wayzzz!" Marsha and Sherlock peered into the darkness as the buzzing faded into the distance.

Luvva Dove had found the ring under some dust sheets inside the removal van. At that very moment, she was dashing back with it held safely in her beak.

Harvey Hedgehog uncurled himself as Luvva Dove landed in the rhododendron bush. "You found it!"

Flibber Frog hopped towards Luvva Dove. "Tres bien, but what now my friends?"

"Coo, coo. You mustn't look glum!. It's up to Harvey now, our prickly pal chum!"

Harvey looked scared and curled up into a ball again. "Gulp! m-me? N-No f-fear! I might get trampled on or s-something, Luvva Dove!"

"Coo, come on now Harvey, you must be away! It's up to you to save the day!"

"Oh prickles!" Harvey, popped his nose out to look at Luvva Dove. As nervous as he was, he would do anything for his friends. "I suppose I'll do it for you, but if I get caught I'll be in a jolly bad mood!" With that, he scuttled off across the lawn.

Flibber Frog frowned. "Madame Dove! Why send le hedgehog? I could 'ave done le job instead!"

"Coo, coo, how true! But to make Harvey brave is something we must do!"

Harvey scampered to the old ivy-covered porch at the back of the cottage. He quickly dropped the ring, then he gace a squeal of fright. He could hear footsteps approaching. "Ohh, oh! No! If they find me, they might use me as a football!"

Back upstairs, it seemed like hours before they heard Buzzer Bee returning. He struggled out of the hole with O'Blarney Beetle hanging lifeless in his thin, black, hairy arms.

"I guezzz I was too late, Marsha!"

"Oh no!"

Sherlock rushed up to the beetle and peered closely at him through his magnifying glass.

"The window! Get him to the window!" Marsha curled her long tail around him, sped up the curtain and out across the window sill.

Suddenly, O'Blarney began taking great gulpfuls of the cool air. "Begorra! That was a bumpy ride!"

The others breathed a sigh of relief, life just wouldn't be the same without their silly beetle friend.

Adam wandered out of the house, staring gloomily at the floor. His face lit up as he caught sight of the ring.

He was bursting with excitement as he picked it up. "Hurray! I've found it!"

Mrs Berry looked confused as she sat down to dinner with her family later that evening. "You know, I'd swear that ring wasn't there earlier!"

Mr Berry smiled. "Perhaps the fairies brought it!" Adam and Amy burst out laughing.

"Fairies indeed! Next you'll be telling us that animals can talk!"

Basil Bat grumbled to himself. "Hmmph! Little do they know! This house used to be nice and peaceful until they arrived!"

Marsha Mouse looked up at Basil, who was hanging upside-down from a beam in the loft. "Oh, I don't know. Life can get boring if things are too quiet. Now that we have a new family to look after, I think we'll all be in for a lot of fun!"

Text-Based Sound Effects

"Sprooinng! Crummmp! Kerspllatt!" etc., whilst used extensively in almost every other field of comic writing, cannot be included in cassette/book scripts. It's the job of the recording producer to add these on the sound recording. It doesn't sound right to have the narrator reading out sound effects, and it's even more ridiculous to hear one of the actors speaking them, when they could just as easily be recorded authentically using special sound effects records.

Adaptations

Once you become a known and respected cassette/book

writer, you won't always have to start from scratch and create your own story. Instead, you'll be provided with a professionally produced script, written for yet another different media — film. This often arrives from Hollywood, and is usually the original script for an animated cartoon revolving around the character that you're working on. It becomes your job to re-arrange the script to work in cassette/ book format. In a nutshell, you'll simply need to carefully prune away any unnecessary camera directions that litter the script (things like slow pan, or Fred's POV favouring Harry). Normally, the cartoon scripts are too long — most cassette/book adaptations are between 1800 and 2000 words — original animation scripts can be twice this length, so you'll need to do some careful pruning.

The first thing to go should be all the visually orientated dialogue. Screenwriters often include jokes and scenes that only work in visuals — without pictures, nothing makes sense — everything of this nature must be carefully removed. As a guide, read something out to a partner directly from the script. If it doesn't make sense in the audio world, cut it out. This will probably bring you down to something approaching the correct number of words. If it turns out that you've cut out too much, then go back and look at the visual bits again. Can you re-structure any of them to work for "audio only"?

When we're asked to prepare an adaptation, we normally work right through the script from start to finish, then count the words we've written, and cut (or build up) to the required number. The skill in this is something that you can only learn from experience, and you have to be careful not to cut a character's role down so much that they don't portray the image that they should. It's also not a good idea to edit out any humour, unless it's relying on visuals to work.

A word processor is invaluable in this sort of work, making it easy to edit and add bits and pieces as required, without having to retype the whole script every time. In addition, cassette/book editors, like most others, prefer tidy tippex-and-paste-free scripts. Frankly, we wouldn't recommend that anyone tries this particular branch of comic writing without access to a word processor. After all, as soon as you've had a couple of scripts accepted, then you'll be showing a profit!

Chapter Six

Writing Text Stories for Comics

Text stories written for the comic market are NOT the same as those written for the children's book market! You can forget all about the correct English that you learnt at school — this is Wham! Bang! Zzzapp! action and adventure where everything hangs on excitement and fun.

Here's an example of a comic-type text story for the under-fives. Read it through, then we'll analyse it together:

Henry the Hippopotamus wanted to be famous.

"I wish I was famous," Henry sighed, as he sat in the park. "Then everyone would cheer and clap me and say what a clever hippopotamus I am!"

"Why not become a singer?" suggested the man sitting next to him.

Henry thought this was a good idea, and decided to go for singing lessons. But first he wanted to look the part. He put on a long wig (which kept tickling his nose), a pink and green shirt, long drainpipe trousers, and big cowboy boots. He did look silly!

"I do look GRAND!" Henry said as he admired himself in the mirror.

Everybody laughed as he walked down the street but Henry ignored them. "They won't laugh at me when I'm famous!" he thought.

The singing instructor saw Henry approaching. "What a silly looking hippopotamus!" he thought. But he didn't tell Henry this in case he took his money elsewhere.

"Now," said the singing instructor. "Sing after me. Doh! Ray! Mi! Fa! So! La! Ti! Doh!"

"Doh!" bellowed Henry, so loud that the table fell over with a BANG!

"Ray!" Henry sang and the flower vase broke into pieces!

"Mi!" sang Henry, as the singing instructor's cat ran out of the room in fright!

"Fa!" Henry continued and a picture fell off the wall!

"So!" Henry sang louder, and the window pane SHATTERED!

"La!" Henry's voice rang out, shaking the little house to and fro!

"Ti!" Henry sang LOUDER and the chandelier fell down with a CRASH!

"Doh" Henry sang at the top of his voice, and the roof fell in on the singing instructor.

"STOP! STOP!" cried the singing instructor. "You're wrecking my house! You'll never be a singer!"

Henry was sad. "There must be something I can do that will make me famous," he thought.

Henry asked an orchestra conductor if he could join the orchestra.

"All right!" agreed the conductor.

Henry was given a tuba to play. He did feel proud! "Now I'll become famous, and everyone will cheer and clap me!" he thought.

The conductor raised his baton and the orchestra began to play. POM! POM! POM! POM! went the music sweetly. BLAAARRFF! went Henry's tuba as he blew with all his might. The awful noise made the pianist fall off his chair in fright!

The cymbal player dropped his cymbals on the clarinet player's foot!

The clarinet player shouted "OWW!"

This upset the drummer so much that he put his foot through his drum!

BLAAARRFF! went Henry's tuba again. BLAAARRFF! BLAAARRFF! Henry WAS enjoying himself!

"Enough!" cried the conductor, tearing at his hair in rage. "You silly hippopotamus! You're ruining my orchestra! Be off with you!"

Henry choked back a tear. "I only wanted to become famous!" he said sadly.

The pianist took pity on Henry. "Why not try dancing?" he suggested. "That would make you famous!"

76

Henry went to see a dance instructor. He knew that dancers dressed smartly, so he put on a frilly white shirt, and a red bow tie. He did look smart!

"I'll teach you to tap dance!" said the dance instructor. "Watch me first, and then copy my movements!"

Tap! Tap! Tap! Tap! went the dance instructor's feet on the dance floor.

THUMP! THUMP! THUMP! THUMP! THUMP! went Henry's feet. Henry danced so heavily that the floor bounced up and down like a trampoline.

"Stop!" cried the dance instructor, as he fell down on the floor. "You're too big and heavy to be a dancer! Away with you!"

This time, Henry could not help crying. "I'll never be famous!" he said sadly as he walked through the park. "No one likes me!"

Poor Henry, he did feel sad.

SPLASH! Henry looked up as he heard a splash from the river. A little boy had been playing near the bank, and had fallen in.

"Help!" cried the little boy. "I-I can't s-swim!"

Henry leapt into the river. SPLASH! He swam over to the little boy who was very scared. "Don't be scared," said Henry gently. "I'll save you!"

Henry sat the little boy on his back and swam back to the bank. Everyone in the park had watched the rescue.

"HURRAY!" they cheered as Henry climbed out of the water.

"BRAVO!" they clapped as Henry gave the little boy back to his mother. "What a brave hippopotamus you are!"

Newspaper reporters arrived and took pictures of Henry for their newspapers.

Television interviewers arrived and interviewed Henry for their television programmes. Henry was seen by millions of people all over the country.

"How does it feel to be famous?" asked a reporter.

Henry thought for a moment. "It feels . . . NICE!" he said.

"Three cheers for Henry!" everyone shouted.

HIP! HIP! HURRAY! Everybody clapped and cheered.

Henry did feel proud!

Sound Effects

We started this chapter by mentioning a few comic type sounds. Children love KABLAMM! BOOOMM! and other noises. When you're writing a children's book, then this is a strict no-go area, but with comic, that no-go is replaced with anything-goes. As you saw in the Henry Hippo story, we used written sound effects whenever possible. You don't have to spell the effects correctly either — make up your own "new words" for them instead — don't write "splash!" when "Kersploosshhh!" sounds more appropriate (you'll find a whole section of these useful "words" at the back of this book.)

CAPITALS

With an action-packed story, it's often very useful to highlight certain words — words that are louder or more important than the others. Again, with comic derived text stories, this is perfectly permissible — it builds the excitement. Most written sound effects should be typed in capitals, as should any shouts or screams — AARRRGGHHH!!

Exclamation Marks

Go mad with them!!!! Use them all over the place!!! Kids love them! Look back at our story, and you'll notice that an exclamation mark occurs after almost every piece of dialogue. This is another device for building the excitement up — and keeping the children reading. As a writer, anything that maintains the children's attention is VERY valuable — especially when you're writing text stories destined for comics. Why? Because your story, whether commissioned for a comic or an annual, will be surrounded by colourful easy-to-digest picture story strips. Children prefer these infinitely to the text stories because they LOOK more fun. Your text story will be the last thing that they read at the very best. At worst, they won't read it at all. Capitals, sound effects and exclamation marks that leap out of the page at you, make that great wadge of text look like fun!

Stutters

Fear and surprise can be introduced in dialogue by simply adding stutters. Look at the section in the Henry Hippo story where the little boy falls into the river, and you'll see what we m-mean.

Story Structure

Even children's stories for comics need to have all the ingredients of a good adult novel — an absorbing plot, cause and effect, good characters that interweave with each other, a good beginning, middle and ending, and lots of excitement — and perhaps just a touch of sadness somewhere in-between. Many editors also like stories to have some form of message attached to them. For example, if you set a story near a frozen pond, then you should subtly explain the danger of falling through ice in your story, or, if one of your characters has to cross a busy road, then ensure that they stop and follow the correct procedure of looking both ways, not crossing behind parked vehicles etc. We also like to introduce children, through exciting stories, to such topics as looking after their environment, tidiness, caring for others, and other issues which will, hopefully, turn them into nice people. However, if you decide to address these issues, then you must be especially careful not to appear patronising. Children have an extraordinarily keen sense of knowing when they're being "talked down to", and will rebel against you by simply closing the annual or comic. You should, therefore, aim to make your writing appear as transparent as possible — telling a good story, without letting your own prejudices intrude too far.

Furthermore, you've got to make sure you know who you're talking to — or writing for. Obvious? We thought so too — once, but as you become more experienced, you realize that you didn't know children at all. Be honest with yourself — do you know the current playground sayings and expressions? Do you know what pop stars picture adorns your target age group's bedroom walls? Do you know what television programmes children watch? — and what their favourites are? Do you know what the conversation in the playground revolves around? Do you really know children at all? Don't worry, we used to answer "no" to most of those questions, but not now — we've spent many long hours researching, reading, asking and finding out. Television is a good guide to what children like — What groups are on the children's shows? What are the most popular cartoons? What are the most widely advertised toys? etc. Spend a few weeks glued to the box in the early evening, and find out BEFORE you begin writing your comic-text stories — if the nine o'clock news is still YOUR favourite programme after you've finished your research, then forget it — you'd be better off writing for *The Times* — at least you'd know your market. We're sorry to appear so blunt, but we've seen so many people fail for no better reason than they don't know who they're writing for. Anyway, if you're not too disgusted with the way we're treating you, then read on — we'll be nice for a few pages and tell you about structuring your story.

If you're writing for the under fives, then you need to remember that they've only got a limited span of concentration. It's best to keep stories for them to something between 300 and 800 words — even the lower limit can be enough to tell a good yarn — Marvel's Thomas the Tank Engine stories, of which we've written many, are just 360 words long! Also, remember to use simple sentences, repetition, and images that are easy to visualize. These youngsters love to be made to laugh. Also, as adults will be the readers of your work, (tiny tots can't read for themselves just yet) the secret is to make your work appeal to them as well. If you can make them laugh out loud with their children, then you're onto a winner — if you can make the editor who you're trying to sell it to laugh out loud as well, you must be a bloody miracle worker!

With the five to eight year olds, your stories can be made a little bit longer, perhaps between 800 and 1000 words. At this age group, the children are just beginning to read for themselves, whereas with the under fives, it's going to be more of a "listen with mother" affair. Also, the five to eight age groups begin to take things more seriously and question ridiculous things happening within the story.

The eight to twelve year olds offer you the chance to

lengthen your stories to somewhere between 1000 and 3000 words. This age group is excited by adventure and suspense. They love to be able to identify with the hero. And all children like to be scared a little as they read their stories — but don't terrify them just yet!

Henry Hippo — Structure Analysis

Our Henry Hippo story was written with the under fives in mind. It's a well-rounded story with three main episodes — which is about right for this age group. These are Henry wanting to be a pop star, Henry playing in the orchestra, and Henry making the heroic rescue of the little boy from the river. We've made the hero (a hippopotamus?) a character that the children can believe in. The overriding theme is a common one — triumph over adversity. We've made up a whole train of funny disasters that the child can easily picture in their mind's eye, and carefully presented a whole host of bizarre images that appeal to the very young. Young children are keen on the sound of the human voice, and so we've made intelligent use of this medium — the reader had got to get through so many sound-effects that they can't help but have fun when reading it aloud to their children. The essential happy ending is there too — and you thought we'd just banged it out quickly!

Another point to note is the beginning — Henry the Hippopotamus wanted to be famous — that's our opening. Just a simple statement, then straight into the action. No messing about with long introductory paragraphs — grab the reader's attention with some dialogue as soon as possible, then maintain that interest through to the end — that's our policy, and it should be yours too.

If you didn't know already, all speech should begin and end with speech marks — these things " — and every time there's a change of speaker, you should start a new paragraph. A complete change of scene necessitates a new section, and this should be separated from the last by an extra line of space. Your work must be double spaced — that means arranging for a blank line to occur between each one that you type. This gives our friendly editors the chance to entirely deface your story with their blue pens, chopping and changing things around to their liking. You should also make sure that whatever you send out to editors is typed, and that you have retained a copy. Quite often, we find that to save time, an editor will phone up and ask you to do some quick alterations to your story — you feel a right prat if he's got the only copy, and you have to ask him to send it back first — especially if he's just said "you'll obviously have a copy there, won't you?"

It's easy for new writers to the medium to misjudge the pace of their story, either plodding through the first three quarters, and then, realising that there's not many words left, cramming all the action and excitement in the last quarter — the children wouldn't have read that far so you needn't have bothered — or, filling the start of the story with copious thrills and spills and a healthy dose of excitement, then finding that the happy ending is looming up, even though there's still three quarters of the story to go, padding things out to the required amount of words. Neither of these work — although at least in the second example, the children will read to the middle before turning to one of the comic strips.

Both of these problems can be avoided by carefully splitting up the story into equally spaced word groups — eg; 300 for the beginning, 300 for the middle, and 300 for the end. But this can only be taken as a guide — if you follow the rule too precisely, then your stories will sound too pre-planned. Also, the beginning will have to be very exciting indeed to warrant 300 words, and endings need to be exceptionally happy to be strung out for the same. The best compromise is to tailor your sectional word count to the subject and story that you're working on — but plan the count BEFORE you start — otherwise it could be too late, and you'll be faced with an unavoidable, boring re-write.

Within each section, you'll now be in a better position to plan the action, and know how long you can devote to each exciting episode. Can that fight between the superhero and the villain still last for 200 words, or will some of the dialogue have to be cut? Should I cut that introductory paragraph down a bit and keep the whole fight scene in? Ultimately, these things have to be your own decision — they're what make you a good writer, but an element of pre-planning can greatly assist in making the RIGHT decisions at these times — a word processor can also be a great friend in these times of trauma. Most have a facility called copy and paste. You can specify a piece of text that you want to get rid of, edit it from the page, and store it in the computer's memory. Then, if it turns out that you do need it after all, press paste and pop it back into your story.

Text stories are great fun to do, and although there's not an enormous potential market for them, they can provide you with a useful regular income.

Style Bible — Superheroes

When you're working on licensed characters, the comic company will normally be able to supply you with some photocopied pages which give you essential background information. Without this, it's almost impossible to produce a story — although we have managed it a couple of times. To give you a chance to get some practice in, we've provided a style bible for our own characters, Doctor Decay, and Tidal Force. We suggest that you try to produce a text story and a comic strip from the information given.

Tidal Force

Tidal Force is the super-hero. He has the power to control the oceans. He has the use of aqua-blasts which can emanate from his fingertips. When underwater, no creature or mechanical object can keep up with him. He possesses a strength thirty times that of any human being. This protects his body from water pressure when deep diving.

Above the waterline, Tidal Force still has the same special powers, and uses the moisture within the atmosphere to regenerate his strength. He can call upon the elements to assist him when required, and derives great power from the moon — as it affects the tides on earth.

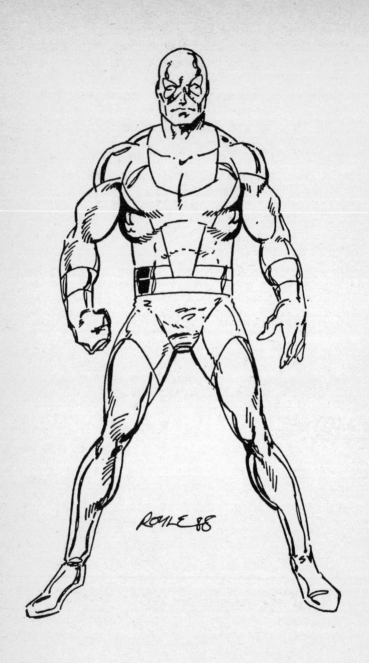

Doctor Decay

The evil doctor has an awesome power — anything that he grasps with his bare hands turns to dust. Human beings can turn to skeletons at his merest touch. He is evil beyond bounds, and will stop at nothing to gain control of the World. Tidal Force is his arch-rival. Most of the time, Doctor Decay wears thick gloves — to stop HIMSELF being turned to decaying dust!

Chapter Seven

Sending It Off

So, you've read our book, done all your homework, and come up with what you think is an acceptable script — acceptable, that is, to both you, and your intending editor. The next thing to do is send it off and hope for the best. However, before you do that, there are a few other points worth checking. Collectively, they will give your manuscript a better chance of metamorphosing into a typeset page read by thousands.

The biggest enemy of the novice comic writer is the editor's waste paper basket — it's there that many scripts end their days. But editors are not ogres (some of them are quite nice!) however, you should know by now that they are very busy people, and will often reject things because they don't *look* like they're going to be any good: A tattered secondhand, screwed up manuscript wouldn't tempt us much first thing on a Monday morning — would it tempt you? But that's exactly what many editors are faced with. So rule number one — always ensure that your manuscript arrives flat, tidy and unfolded in a good quality envelope. It's tempting to re-send a returned manuscript out again to another editor without re-typing it, but this is false economy in the long run — the editor isn't stupid, and will instantly recognise a secondhand deal.

Rule number two relates, not to the appearance of the paper itself, but to how the work is actually written on it. Some editors don't like dot matrix computer submissions at all. Apparently, they find them hard to read. They prefer "letter quality" submissions. These are usually produced by a typewriter or computer printer of the "daisywheel" type. It's best to fit these with a carbon ribbon, (double strike lasts longer than normal) as this produces a beautiful black print that's clear and very easy to read. It also looks more professional.

The pages that form the manuscript should be set out in a particular way too. We've never bothered with title pages, preferring to start with the title on the first page of the manuscript itself, centralized. Some typewriters, and all word processors, have an auto-centralizing feature that's very useful for this — on others, you need to do the task manually using the typewriter's ruler.

Below this we scroll down two lines and begin. As we've mentioned earlier, manuscripts must be presented using double spacing (an extra blank line between each typed line). In addition, you should ensure that there is a margin on both sides of the paper of about 1-1½ inches, this makes any editorial corrections with the dreaded blue pen easy.

Headers and footers on each page are very useful, especially if the manuscript pages become accidentally detached in a busy office. On our comic manuscripts, we begin each page, except the title one, with a header that gives the name of the story. This is then separated from the main body of text by a line stretching right across the page.

At the bottom of each page, we arrange for a footer to appear. This carries our business name, Creative Imaginations, our office phone numbers, and also the number of that particular page of the manuscript. Like the header, this footer is divided from the bulk of the text by another line stretching right across the page.

The important task of headers and footers can become very tedious, and upset the creative flow of thought quite easily — especially if you have to stop and type them out for each page. Thankfully, the good old word processor saves the day again. Once you've set the templates up for these headers and footers before you begin, they occur automatically throughout the manuscript, with even the page numbering being carried out by the computer.

Right justification is another device which can be used to make your manuscripts look just that little bit more professional — and consequently stand out from the rest of the pile. This is where all of the words on the right hand side of the page finish in line with each other, rather like the way a finished book is printed. Again, this is best achieved with the help of a word processor, although some of the best typewriters now have this facility too. The trouble is, a good typewriter with these facilities, costs much more than a modern word processor. This book, and most of our output, is produced on a machine called an Amstrad PCW 9512. It's a complete system with keyboard, disc drive (for storing data), TV monitor screen, and daisywheel printer. At the time of writing it costs well under £600 for the whole system. The typewriters that we used cost almost as much, and were many times less versatile. We're not suggesting that you *Must* have a word processor to become a successful comic writer, we're just pointing out that they're not as expensive as you think, and that they are useful.

Obviously it's no good simply sending off a manuscript in an envelope and hoping for a good result — there is an element of salesmanship involved. Your hard work should be accompanied by a brief covering letter. This should match the standard of your manuscript, and be properly typed, preferably on headed notepaper. Your address should be on the right, aligned with the right hand margin, whilst your recipient's address should follow it on the left. Under this should be today's date, and then something like this — if it's a speculative submission.

Please find enclosed, for consideration for publication in . . . . . . a story/comic strip entitled . . . . . . revolving around . . . . . . (character used).

Should it be suitable then I would appreciate, in addition to payment at your normal rates, a copy of the issue in which it appears, for my records. If it is unsuitable, then I would be grateful for its return, together with any useful editorial remarks.

The customary SAE is enclosed.

The last five words are the most important — without an SAE, your manuscript has much less chance of being returned if it's unsuitable. You have to consider how many scripts are sent to editorial offices a week. Think of how much money each office would have to spend on postage if they had to pay for return postage on every unsuitable item that came in. It's also very useful for the editor if you specify the amount of words that the manuscript runs to (if it's a text story). Editors have specifically sized spots in their comics to fill, and like to know at a glance what they've got, to fill those spaces at short notice.

A returned manuscript could be a very useful aid in your development. You should learn from each rejection — Are there any editorial remarks on the manuscript? Does the covering letter ask you if you have any further material? Is it a "standard letter", or has the editor sent you a personal one? (he must have thought you were worth it if he did).

Many hours of wasted effort can be avoided by simply making a telephone call to the editor *Before* starting work at all. Be brief, explain your idea, and ask if they could use it. Be friendly but professional — editors can't be bothered with gibbering creeps! Working in this way, the editor will be expecting your work, and look out for it when it arrives. To further ensure this desirable state of affairs, it's a good idea to put your name on the envelope. Incidentally, your address should always be written on the back flap so that, if the packet is lost, the Post Office at least know where to return it. The covering letter should mention that you've already spoken to the editor on the phone, and that he/she suggested you should send in your script.

Copyright and Contracts

With most publishing deals, the writer gets an advance, followed later by a royalty which is a percentage of the cover price of every book sold. The writer also retains copyright in his or her work — with comics, this is all out of the window — forget it! When you write a comic strip based on a famous character, you will be paid a once-only fee and that, we're unhappy to report, will be that. You see, although you've created the story, you've got no rights to the characters who populate it — they're owned by the comic company, or quite often, licensed from major toy manu-facturers, or even character creation companies, like ourselves.

90

Payment

Okay, so now you've written your comic script, sent it off, and it's been accepted by an editor. Congratulations! Now you deserve to know about payment, and the certain drawbacks associated with writing comics in Britain.

Scripts are bought outright by comic companies. This means that you have no control over your work once it has been accepted. The copyright in the story, and, if you have created a new series, the characters, too, automatically become the property of the company concerned. You receive a once-only payment, no matter how many times the story is reprinted, either at home or abroad — and there's a good chance of the latter occurring. If it turns out that the characters you have created become immensely popular, and subsequently begin appearing on merchandise, such as toys, or even made into a feature film, all the profits go to the comic companies, you receive *Nothing!*

This is an alarming state of affairs, but one which unfortunately exists with all the comic companies in Britain. (The American firms do pay royalties: see *Writing The American Comic Strip*). We all live in hope that these matters will change, but the heads of the companies that count are, understandably, adverse to change on this matter, as they feel that it could ultimately cost them considerably more money to produce their publications. We feel that, if you create something, you should be able to maintain a commercial interest in it. All comic writers are pushing for change, but not too hard for fear they will get fired! Change will come, one day, but don't hold your breath waiting. A policy of "grin and bear it" currently works best.

Our advice to all writers working for British comics is this: only write for established comic series. Don't create your own series or characters unless you are willing to give away all rights to them, and perhaps see a comic company make a big profit out of your ideas. Keep all your good ideas for the American markets, and for books.

If we may be so bold as to venture a solution to the above — why not give writers the chance of making a decision? — retain copyright, and be paid royalties only, or sell on a buy-out basis (the current way). As things stand, writers feel they should hold back their best material — which, in the long run, is bad for them, the company concerned, and the reader!

A further criticism (sorry!) of British comic companies is that only two of the "big five" print author's names on published stories. Fleetway provide credits on a select few titles, and it's left to Marvel to uphold the writer's rights. They deserve praise for using credits on almost all their titles. One of the weakest editorial excuses we've heard for not giving by-lines is that "we're concerned that other (higher paying?) companies will poach our best writers and artists." The real truth is unfortunately that many editors delight in keeping their writers "under their thumbs", and make them feel grateful for any work they are "allowed" to submit. Again, this is changing gradually, but there's still a long, hard road ahead.

Payment is per page of strip, unlike for text, where you are paid per 1000 words. Page rates vary at each company. D. C. Thomson pay the lowest rates, but they do encourage new writers, and their editors make real efforts to work with contributors in a bid to strengthen story ideas, (one of us began our writing career with Thomson's humour comics). London Editions pay slightly better, while Fleetway, TV Times Publications (who publish Look-In), and Marvel have varying page rates, which are on a scale determined by the experience of the writer, and the type of stories required.

Invoices

All companies apart from D. C. Thomson require invoices. To submit an invoice, simply buy a suitable book from any Post Office or stationers, then, ensuring that a carbon sheet is in place, enter your name, address and the title of the comic, plus the story title. In the column provided, write how much they have agreed to pay you.

Payment will either come on acceptance, or on publication — and sometimes up to a month afterwards. D. C. Thomson and London Editions generally pay within a month of acceptance. With Marvel, it's a month after invoices have been issued, whilst Fleetway pay on publication, or soon afterwards. If you become prolific and respected in the industry, you'll end up with as much work as you can possibly handle, and make a reasonable living into the bargain.

Chapter Eight

Partners and Profits

Partners — Pros and Cons

There are many advantages to writing in tandem with a partner. For a start, it's much more fun than working alone. Writers have a strange habit of locking themselves away from all forms of distraction while they are working. The trouble is, they're locking out the inspiration the outside world can provide. It's not surprising then, that so-called "writer's block" becomes a real fear with these people.

A writing partnership can strengthen your output, making ideas flow faster and more imaginatively. It's easy to find yourself working twice as hard as you would do on your own. From a commercial standpoint, this is great, because it means that twice as much material is produced, giving you twice as much chance of selling.

Partnerships can be likened to any long-standing relationship. You have your good and bad days. There will be times when you can't wait to start an exciting new project, and times when you can't stand the sight of each other. However, a good partnership is one that can survive the worst and enjoy the best.

I think that Brian Cooke sums up a partnership best in his invaluable book, *Writing Comedy for Television*. He says: "I can't deny that there is enormous satisfaction in creating a whole show on your own, or writing a good sketch without anybody's help. At the same time, of it goes wrong, it's quite nice to have somebody to share the blame."

Managing the Money

You need to have a plan detailing what you want to achieve.

94

I suggest that you split the year into four, three-monthly quarters, and set a target figure for income in each quarter. Make it realistic — but not too easy. It's fun then striving for target figures — and it's cause for celebration if you exceed them. A business bank account is also a must. These are easily set up, and this makes it easy to split up all your personal purchases/deposits from your business ones — useful when you make tax returns.

Tax

It's important to keep accounts too — and that's something that scares most people off. But it's easy, all you have to do is write down who gives you money, when, what for, and how much. This forms the basis of what you supply to the taxman at the end of the year — or rather, every April. You are allowed to offset earnings against anything that you've spent money on, such as stock, heating, lighting, telephone etc. — in fact, almost everything purchased in connection with the running of your business. The difference between the two figures is the amount on which you'll be taxed. Your tax office will give you further information (they're quite friendly people really). If you don't want the hassle of tax returns, then you could engage an accountant.

A sole trader or partnership has to notify the inspector of taxes on form 41G that a business has been established. The Inland Revenue have published a useful booklet (IR28), called Starting In Business, which can be obtained from your tax office or from the Small Firms Service. If the business makes a profit in its first year, then tax will be payable, although it will not be collected until some time after the end of the first year. However, it's a good idea to put aside some money to meet a possible tax demand as you earn it. Losses may be offset against taxable profits in the following two years.

National Insurance

You'll also need to sort out your own National Insurance

contributions. However, if you don't think you're going to make much money in the first year, then you can apply for an exemption certificate. Normally you'll have to fork out for class 2 contributions — bought as stamps as the Post Office. You can find out more about NI contributions from your local Department of Health and Social Security, there are a number of leaflets dealing with the subject available at these offices. The most useful ones are N41 — National Insurance Guide for the Self-Employed, and NI27 — People with Small Earnings from Self Employment (information on exemption certificates).

Setting Up a Partnership

This needn't involve a lot of hassle. All you need to do is visit a bank and apply to open up a joint business bank account. To make money easy to handle, you simply arrange that all cheques must be signed by BOTH parties — that means that neither partner can touch any of the business money without the other's permission — simple. We've got an account of this nature with the Co-Op bank — they were very helpful.

Enterprise Allowance Scheme

It's quite possible that you could be eligible for a £40 per week grant to help get you started in business. There's a scheme available, run by the Manpower Service Commission. You can find out more about it by contacting your local jobcentre, or by dialling 100, speaking to the operator and asking for Freephone Enterprise. So what's the catch? Well, you need to have been unemployed for eight weeks or more, and must be in receipt of unemployment, and/or supplementary benefit. You also need to be able to raise £1000 yourself, be between 18 and 65 years of age, and be willing to work a minimum of 37 hours per week. If you're keen to take the plunge into writing in a serious way, then it's easy to make yourself eligible, and you'd be mad not to take advantage of such a valuable offer — we wish the Enterprise Allowance

Scheme had been available when we started. We used to go for weeks without a penny, and struggle to afford typewriter ribbons — come to think of it, we still do sometimes — but that's life I suppose!

Chapter Nine

Write Answers

The nearest that we can come to helping you face-to-face with your work, is to anticipate some of your questions.

1. Do I need a literary agent if I'm working for comics?

No. Comic editors will deal directly with you, and literary agents are only interested in people who write books, not comics. We've got an agent, but that's because we do lots of other writing besides comics — like this book for instance.

2. So why is it that agents don't want to deal with anything apart from books?

An agent works on commission — that is, they'll take a percentage of anything that they handle for you. The going rate is 10%. This percentage can make the agent quite a lot of money if you are embarking on a full length work targeted at a major publisher. However, the profit from the one off sale of several comic strips to a comic company would yield only peanuts for the busy agent, and take up just as much of their time. They've got to ensure that their time is used cost-effectively.

3. Who chooses the artists to work on my scripts — do I have any say?

The editor will decide on the artist to illustrate your strip story. Writers do have artists they prefer to work with, and may occasionally suggest an artist to an editor. But the editor must have the final decision, based on a variety of factors: Is the artist suitable for your story? (Artists who can produce exquisite illustrations for young children may be unable to create the required effects needed for a gothic horror story.) Will the artist be able to meet the deadline? (some artists are notoriously slow.) Does the artist charge too much per page? Is there a more suitable artist available? The writer cannot expect to be aware of all of these factors. Therefore, he or she has little say in who illustrates his story — and rightfully so.

4. How much am I likely to earn from writing for comics?

This all depends on which country you are working for. In Britain, the page rate can be quite low (at D. C. Thomson, especially), while other companies pay what some writers consider to be a reasonable amount. The average, at the time of writing, is about £20 per page. However, unlike all other industries, and except for I.P.C., British comics are the only place where you do not receive an annual increase. The last page rate rise that we had was three years ago. In contrast, in America, the average pay for a new writer is $1000 per complete comic.

5. Do established comic writers get higher pay than beginners?

It depends on the company. In Britain, some companies respect their top writers and will pay them a higher rate than that given to beginners. Others lump all writers together, whatever their experience, and pay them the same rate. America, as seen above, treats their top writers well, and so they should, without them the companies wouldn't sell as many comics as they do!

6. Can I make more money writing for the American market?

Of course! America is built and survives on the pretext that money is everything. American comics will pay you a fee for your story, and if sales of the comic exceed a given total, then you'll also receive royalties on every copy. There are some very rich comic writers in America. (A number of British writers now work solely for American comics.)

7. Has a comic editor the right to change my scripts, and should I permit it?

Yes. Sometimes slight changes are required, and usually the editor knows the character (especially licensed ones) better than you do. Frankly, we don't worry about changes made to our work — the editor can do exactly as he pleases

— as long as we get paid! One of the most frequent changes an editor will make is with regard to your title. Usually, editors are able to think up much better titles than the writer, and have the advantage of knowing what their readership wants. It's normally only amateurs who complain about changes being made to their work — we feel that it's both childish and unprofessional to complain about a few changes — you should feel that way too.

8. Will I be contacted prior to any editorial changes?

Normally, no — unless an editor wants to query something with you. Scripts can be completely restructured and re-written by an editor or staff writer, and you have no say in the matter. This is especially true of new writers. Hopefully, your script will not require major surgery anyhow.

9. If I only sell the occasional comic strip story, do I have to declare it to the taxman?

You should declare ALL your writing sales — the publication that you've appeared in will have declared its payments to the tax people, so they'll probably know about your new income, even if you think they don't. It's easy to keep sales records — and just as easy to keep records of outgoings too, read on . . .

10. How can I legally minimize my tax liability?

When you begin to make regular sales to comics, then you'll have to start paying tax on what you earn. This is where it becomes very important to keep a careful record of your expenses. Make sure you obtain a receipt for each item connected with writing that you buy. Some of the things that Tax Inspectors will normally allow against earnings include:

Postage — buy books of stamps and keep the stubs as proof for tax purposes, and don't forget to include envelopes too. You should also be able to claim for headed notepaper, carbons, typewriter ribbons, labels, pens, pencils and even bottles of Tipp-Ex — though don't use too much of this stuff, or you won't be friends with your editors for long.

Phone calls are also allowable, as are travelling expenses when you are forced to go hundreds of miles to meet an editor for five minutes. If you can justify it, then you can claim for any payments made to your "helpers" — a good example of this may be when you get your wife/husband or girlfriend/boyfriend to type up your scripts ready for submission.

You can also claim on the cost of the services of an accountant, and subscriptions to writing magazines, and even — subject to negotiation with your tax inspector — a portion of the cost of running your home, if it's where you work from. This may include heating, lighting and electricity, and can also extend to the running of your car. You can even claim the cost of this book!

Before you begin your comic writing career, contact your local tax office and arrange a meeting with your area's inspector. Most of them are surprisingly friendly people, keen to assist you in your struggle through the tax maze.

11. What is a kill fee, and can I demand it?

It's a payment that should be provided when publications "mess you about". If an editor writes to you after you've submitted a script, and tells you that it has been accepted but held for some future date, then you have basically entered into a contract. If the editor changes his mind, or gets replaced, and the script is surplus to requirements for some reason or another, then the writer is supposed to be entitled to some compensation for wasted work. The trouble is, comic companies don't see it that way, and if you ask for a kill fee, then you'll probably never work for them again — it's not fair, is it?

12. Why do some comic writers go under pen names?

For a variety of reasons. Prolific writers who receive credits on their work, are sometimes asked by editors to create pen names, so that it doesn't look as if the comic has been written by one person. Other writers who are using comics merely as a stepping stone to higher literary forms of writing, go under pen names so that they will not be recognised.

13. How many people will be reading my comic story when it's published in Britain?

Most publishers work out their readership (as opposed to

how many copies are actually sold) by taking the circulation figure of their publication, and multiplying it by three. It's considered that children share their comics with at least one or two friends. Not a scientific calculation — we never shared our comics with anyone — but it seems to work. So, find out the circulation figure of the comic that you're working on, and you'll know the average readership. It's nice when you find out that the comic you're writing for may be read by in excess of half a million people!

14. Will I always get my name on the story, or is this a rare luxury?

This depends on the company that you're working for. We think that you should get your name on everything you write — you do in America, but they respect THEIR writers!

15. Can a new comic writer break into the business — or is it virtually impossible?

If you can write, then you can be a writer, it's as simple as that. But, like any other skill, you've got to serve an apprenticeship first. With writing, this training is easy — you just write. Weekly, you'll notice yourself improving. This is a process that can be speeded up by researching as many comic-based publications as you can. Many "new" ideas are in fact borrowed from established favourites — there's only a certain amount of ways that Spider-Man can sock it to the baddies! Editors of comics are always on the look-out for promising newcomers, but it's important that your approach, and your script, is professional, and is laid out correctly on the page.

16. Am I too old to write for children's comics?

No, you're never too old, but you must keep up with current children's trends, and really understand the comic concept. There are many successful comic writers who are in their fifties and beyond — comic writing keeps you young — zap! Kapoww!

17. I don't know if my short scripts are any good. Will an editor tell me what he thinks? If not, then how do I find out?

Editors are often nice people who want to encourage new

talent into the industry. If your script has potential, they may spend some time explaining what you are doing wrong, and how you could put it right. If your story is atrocious, they'll also tell you that, and perhaps even venture to suggest that you find another medium to work in (like pottery!) Some editors will reply to unsolicited scripts, others won't. It depends on how busy they are, and how much they care.

18. After I have submitted a script, how long should I wait before querying if I haven't heard anything?

Wait at least a month. Editors are very busy people. They can receive a dozen or more unsolicited scripts every week. After they've done all of the jobs that they are required to do in producing a weekly or monthly publication (and some editors work on more than one title at a time), they will try to find time to look over your script). Amazingly, in the circumstances, most scripts are replied to within a fortnight, unless you've sent your submission at a very busy period in the comic calendar.

19. Should I send an invoice with my script?

As a beginner, we would advise you not to send an invoice unless the editor has specifically requested one, and you've discussed an agreed payment rate beforehand. However, in the USA, you are always expected to issue an invoice with your work — they're very much more business orientated over there. When you're established in Britain, you could begin issuing invoices (we do). It often means that you get paid much earlier.

20. Do I have to count the words that I write?

Yes, if you're writing text stories. The editor will usually give you a specific amount of words in which to tell your tale. You must get as close as possible to this target figure. A certain amount of space will have been allocated for your story (if it's been commissioned) — too few words will mean a blank-looking page, and too many words will mean that the story has to be set in a smaller, more compact typeface than originally planned — not good for encouraging young children to read.

With comic strips, the amount of words is less important,

but you shouldn't have more than two people speaking in each panel — and remember, no matter how good the letterer is, he can't be expected to cram too many words into a small speech balloon. Some comic strips have a couple of lines of text underneath each panel. The length of these short text passages is often critical, and has to be counted in actual characters and spaces, not just words. If you're asked to submit such a script, check the exact requirements first with your intended editor. Copy that is good AND fulfils the required length stands much more chance of being accepted.

21. How much dialogue against narrative should there be in a comic text story?

This depends largely on the target age group for the story. The youngest like more dialogue, whilst the older children prefer more of an even mix, with narrative sometimes taking precedence over the dialogue. It should be pointed out that, in America, there are NO text stories in comics.

22. How long after my story is accepted will I have to wait before publication?

Again, it depends. A story for a weekly paper may appear between six weeks and six months after it has been accepted. Stories for annuals are sometimes written a year ahead! And not all companies will send you complimentary copies of the comic that your work appears in, so you have to keep careful watch.

23. When should I send in a seasonal story?

At least three months before the actual date of the festivities. It is no good sending in a wonderful Christmas story in late December. By then the comics will be working up to the Valentine's Day issues. You must learn to think ahead. We are usually writing our Christmas stories while sunning ourselves on the beach (well, almost!)

24. How can I tell what sort of story is required by a comic?

You have to read a comic to understand what sort of stories are needed. Editors still get romance stories sent to war comics, and sci-fi epics submitted to publications for the

under fives. Do your homework before you send ANY-
THING off.

25. Is there any chance of writing non fiction for comics?
   No. Features are written by staff writers; there may be an
occasional feature that you could sell to an annual, but this
is very unlikely. Where comics are concerned, stick to
stories.

Appendix One

A Glossary of Comic Terms

When you begin to write for comics, much of the technical jargon can seem strange. What is a 'splash panel?'. Where should the 'logo' be situated? At first, it all seems like a confusing maze that only professional comic writers understand. To succeed, you've got to become that professional, and so it's worth taking a little time to learn this new language. It can make all the difference to your chances — an editor will recognise an experienced comic scriptwriter from the amateur and choose the former every time, so you need to get it right.

To help you become accustomed to 'comic talkese', CREATIVE IMAGINATIONS are happy to give the following glossary of comic terms. Learn them well. There may be a test later!

Action

A prime ingredient to most comic strip stories. Action must be used naturally, to enhance and progress a plot, and not slapped in willy-nilly to pad out a story. You don't have to resort to scenes of violence — action is best described as something that happens — from kissing in the back seat of the movies on a Saturday night, to beating up the bad guys — which is an integral part of the story.

Action/Adventure Strip

The mainstay of the boy's comic, featuring a hero (or heroes) triumphing over evil, to save the world from destruction. Not all comics feature 'world-shattering' plots, many are just exciting adventures, full of suspense. There are many different categories of 'action/adventure strip': crime, thrillers, super heroes, horror, detective, westerns, and science fiction.

Animal Strips

Sometimes called the 'funny animal' strip, because the majority of the stories are humorous in content. Still used occasionally in Britain, an animal comic strip is one that features an animal, or group of animals, as the leading characters. The stories may or may not be supported by a human cast. The animals are usually able to talk, walk and act like humans. (Check out KORKY THE CAT, THE GET ALONG GANG, PUP PARADE, etc.) Others keep their animal traits and the stories revolve around recognisable human settings. (The most famous in Britain being FRED BASSET.) Sadly, animal stories seem to be declining, except in newspaper strips. Apart from a few titles in Marvel's STAR COMICS, they are almost non-existent in America.

Annual

1. A hardback edition of a British comic, published once a year, at Christmas, with both new and reprinted material. 2. A once-yearly edition of a popular American comic book, twice the page size of the normal monthly title.

Artwork

A comic strip script is broken down into a number of sequential visual panels, drawn by an artist. Artwork is drawn one and a half or twice 'up', (one and a half or twice the size) it will appear in a comic.

Assistant Editor

The editor's lackey. Be nice to him 'cos he's the person most likely to be promoted to editor.

Back-Up Story

The first story in a comic is called a 'lead' story, though in Britain this does not mean it is the most popular. (The favourite comic strips tend to be placed in the colour centre pages.) With a number of strip series in the publication, there is no real 'back-up' story as such, in the majority of British comics. (This is set to change in some comics in the near future.). American comics occasionally use 'back-up' stories; these are shorter than the lead story (generally around eight pages in length), and sometimes feature characters from the leading comic strip. They are a useful way for writers to break into a new market.

Background (B/G)

The background of a picture. Usually scenery, like buildings or fields.

Balloon

The white balloons used to denote dialogue or thinking, and coming from the lips, or just above the heads, of comic characters.

Believeability

Everything you write must conceivably be able to happen, whether it's talking animals or super-heroes flying overhead.

Bible

Contains full background information on a licensed series.

Bi-Monthly

A comic that is published every other month.

Bi-Weekly

Also known as 'fortnightly'. A comic that appears every other week.

Birds-Eye View

Cinematic technique to explain to an artist that you want a picture drawn from looking down at a scene from a higher elevation.

Black and White (B&W)

A story printed in black and white.

Box

Synonym for caption box. When writing script directions some writers prefer to use the term BOX instead of CAPTION.

Cameo

A limited appearance by a recognisable character in another comic strip series that is not their own. They may only appear for a few panels, or a couple of pages at most. This is most common in American super-hero comics. Cameos should only really be done with characters from the same company.

Caption (CAP)

Usually placed in the upper left hand side of a panel. The caption is the area where the narrative of a story is placed in a comic strip.

Cartoon

A humorous comic strip.

Cartoonist

An artist who draws cartoons.

Cartoon Strip

A humourous newspaper comic strip.

Character(s)

The fictional people who populate the panels of a comic strip.

Characterisation

Believable characters, good and bad, are made up of their little quirks and habits. Each character should be a separate individual, with their own feelings, needs, desires, motives, etc. Remember, good characterisation creates believeable individuals that readers can relate to.

Cinematic Technique

The best way to write instructions for an artist when scripting a comic strip is to imagine you are writing the screenplay for a film or television programme. Using cinematic jargon such as POV (point of view), close-up, and fade-out will help you to visualise how a strip will look when drawn. Your comic strip will look much more exciting if drawn from different viewpoints.

Conflict

The obstacles a character has to surmount in the course of trying to reach their goal.

Close-Up

Art instruction. Most effective for emphasising detail of a subject, facial expressions, and gestures. Useful for a close view or examination of a subject.

Colourist

An experienced person who colours in the artist's drawings.

Comic

A publication that features stories told in comic strip form. The name comes from the first types of comics published, which were humorous in nature.

Comic Book

The American term for comics.

Comics Code Authority (CCA)

In the Fifties, American comics were considered 'bad' for children, due to an excess of violence and bondage scenes. The Comics Magazine Association of America created The Comics Code Authority and drew up a set of regulations for comics to abide by. The CCA consists of a board selected from all the main companies. All comics that meet these standards may display the CCA seal of approval on their covers. In recent times there has been a change in the outlook of comic publishers. While most editors within the industry think the Code ought to be updated on a regular basis in standing to what is acceptable to current social trends, they sometimes find that it's too weak to suit today's comics. Whilst companies will not intentionally print controversial material, there are a number of comics now used for an 'adult' readership. These cannot abide by the Code's rules. These comics often feature a disclaimer on the cover, stating that the material featured in the comics is for a 'mature audience'.

Continuity

A comic strip serial; a story that is not complete, but is told in weekly or monthly parts.

Crossover

An American device, where a recognisable character from one series appears with the lead character(s) in a different series, for the entire story. (Different from 'cameo'.) Also known as the 'guest-star(s)', or 'guest-shot'.

Daily Strip

A comic strip, usually of three panels, which appears daily in a newspaper.

Debut

The first appearance of a comic strip character.

Dialogue

What comic strip characters speak, as shown in 'speech balloons'. Dialogue is used to display character and further the plot. No more than 25 words to a balloon.

Distance

Art instruction. Not in the foreground. i.e. "In the distance, we see Mount Vesuvius erupting. . . ."

Dream Sequence

Scalloped panels used to denote daydreaming and nightmares.

Editor

Your immediate boss when selling work to a company.

Editor-in-Chief

The editor's boss.

Embellisher

An inker who works on brief pencils of a layout artist.

Emotion

Anger, fear, love, humility, courage, suspicion, loneliness, hate, despair, joy, gratitude, amusement, pride, etc. What the character is feeling.

End

THE END. The last words you write after the finish of your 'best-selling' comic script. It indicates to a half-asleep editor that there is no more to come.

Episode

One installment of an on-going serial.

External Shot

When you require a script direction to move from inside to outside, you ask for an 'external shot'. i.e. "External shot of the building. . . ."

Establishment Shot

Setting the scene for the events.

Fade-In/Fade-Out

An instruction to the artist to create a visual impression of a picture coming in or out of view.

Flashback

A useful device in comic stories, enabling you to look back on a scene from the past. Mainly used in American comic books.

Footnote (or Foot Panel)

A caption box that is placed along the bottom right hand side of the final panel of a strip, usually to invite readers to buy the next issue to see how their heroes will triumph over adversity.

Foreground (F/G)

The part of a scene that is in the very front of a picture.

Fortnightly

A comic that is published every other week.

Frame

Another term for 'panel'.

Frame-Within-A-Frame

Sometimes a story may call for a smaller frame (or panel) featuring a character or scene, to be displayed inside a larger frame.

Headshot

Art direction, used when only the head of a character is to be shown.

Holiday Special

Published in the summer and winter, special editions of popular British comic titles.

Humour

A nice ingredient to include in even the most dramatic story. The best adventure stories are filled with humorous touches.

Humour Strip

A funny, or comedic comic strip.

Illo

Short term for illustration.

Independent Comics

Also known as 'alternative' comics. Comics published by small companies. There are very few independent companies in Britain.

Inker

A person who inks over the pencilled drawings supplied by an artist. Widely practised in America, it used to be uncommon in Britain, but is growing in the '80s, especially on adventure strips.

Intro

Introduction. The first appearance of a character.

Issue

An edition of a comic. 'Next issue', 'last issue', 'back issue' . . . etc.

Invoice

The chitty you send to a company to get your hard-earned money.

Large Panel

Art direction. When you want an artist to display a visual in a panel that is larger than normal. An effective device to use at the start of a story to catch the reader's attention. See 'Splash'!

Layouts

The rough details — not finished art — of the pencil artist.

Letterer

The person who writes the words on a comic strip.

Licensed Series

A series based on toys, films or television series. Well-known series include *The Care Bears*, *Masters Of The Universe*, *Ghostbusters*, and *Barbie*.

Limited Series

American publishers sometimes bring out a title for a limited number of issues. These usually feature series or characters that would not sell well as an on-going series, but may prove popular for a handful of issues.

Linear View

At the same height as the characters viewpoint.

Logo

The title of a comic, or story.

Long Shot

Art direction. Useful for establishing a setting or location, and for showing objects and figures of great size: spaceships, giants, buildings, etc.

Medium Shot

This type of picture comes in handy when you have action scenes, or for giving a full view of figures or objects, with nothing hidden by the panel borders.

Monthly

A comic that is published once a month.

Narrative

The unspoken words in a comic strip or text story which describe what is happening — basically, everything except dialogue.

Noise

Another term for sound effect. CRAAASSH! SMAAASSH! BAAASSH!

Off-Panel

Something, or someone referred to but not shown in a panel. Characters may speak 'off-panel'.

One-Shot

A comic that is only published once, usually to gauge the reaction of the audience. If it proves popular, it is sure to become a weekly, fortnightly, monthly or bi-monthly title.

Onomatopeia

Our favourite part of a comic strip. 'Sound words' that imitate the noises we hear in real life: BANG! ZZZZZAP! SOCK! POW!

Open Panel

A panel that is not enclosed within a frame. Sometimes called the 'borderless panel'.

Origin

A story which details the history of a character.

Overshoulder Shot

Art direction. Scene viewed from over the shoulder of a character.

Pace/Pacing

The story-flow. Done smoothly there is no jarring effect when shifting to different scenes.

Panning/Panning Back

Drawing back on a scene to show other scene details around the main action.

Panel

A drawing enclosed within a frame; a sequence of these panels make up a comic strip.

Penciller

Also referred to as the artist (though an artist is usually considered to be someone who both pencils and inks their own work). The person who draws the comic strip in pencil, ready for the inker to ink.

Photo Strip

A quirk of British comics. A comic strip story told in a sequence of photographs rather than drawn artwork. A complete failure when it was tried on the Boy's adventure comics, now relegated to the teenage romance titles.

Picture (PIC.)

1. The drawing inside a panel. 2. An art direction. Instead of writing PANEL 1, some writers prefer the term PICTURE 1.

Plot

Without a good, strong plot you don't have a story. A plot has to be interesting and exciting, with the lead character's objective clearly stated. A plot should flow smoothly from beginning to end.

Point of View (POV)

A scene seen through the eyes of a character. i.e. "An empty street, seen from Jack's point of view. . . ."

Publisher

He who supplies the finance which allows the editor to pay you.

Re-Cap

Mainly used in American comics, a story device to remind readers of what happened in the last issue.

Reference Material (REF.)

Anything, from character 'bibles' to photographs, that will help a writer or artist to understand a story better.

Reprint

A comic strip story that is published more than once. In Britain, you receive no additional payment if your story is reprinted.

Revival

The return of an old comic character who has not appeared in a comic for some years. Most popular in the States.

SAE

Stamped addressed envelope. What you should send with your unsolicited script, so that it can easily be returned if found unsuitable by an editor.

Sci-Fi

Sometimes confused as an abbreviation of 'science fiction'. While science fiction stories tend to use plot devices and ideas based on what is believed

115

will be fact in the near future, sci-fi stories are more fantasy orientated. 'Sci-fi' is best described as exploitative science fiction — cheap and inaccurate.

Script

The detailed text, art directions, narrative, dialogue, etc. that makes up a comic strip story.

Scriptwriter

The person who writes the text, narrative and dialogue of a comic strip. That's us!

Sequence

The grouping of panels of artwork or, in Britain, photographs, in chronological order, that make up a comic strip.

Setting

The location or scene of a story.

SF

Science fiction stories.

SFX

Shortened term for 'special effects'.

Shadow

To build tension in a story, it is sometimes effective to show only the shadow of a character, usually the baddie before they are properly introduced.

Silent Strip

Sometimes known as the 'pantomime' strip. A comic strip without any narrative or dialogue, the story is told exclusively in pictures. This is good training for the comic strip writer, and forces you to think in visual terms. There's not much call for it in comics, but is sometimes employed in the newspaper strip.

Silhouette

An effective visual device. A picture of a person or scene showing the outline only, usually black on a white background.

Small Panel/Small Shot

A panel that is smaller than average.

Sound Effect(s)

Another term for 'noise', or onomatopeia. WHACK! ZLAPP! BING!

Special Edition

A comic that does not have a regular frequency. Different from a 'one-shot', as there may be a number of special editions of a title published over the months or years.

Special Effect(s)

Can either be used to denote onomatopeia (sound effects), or an exciting visual effect, like a planet exploding.

Splash Panel

Rarely used in Britain, but popular in the States: The first panel of a comic strip, filling an entire page.

Split Panel

A panel that is split into two or more sections, generally to denote different scenes taking place at the same time — such as a telephone conversation.

Sports Strip

A comic strip based around some aspect of sport, like football or tennis. The famous sporting character in Britain is *Roy Of The Rovers*.

Spread

1. Two sequential pages of a comic or book. 2. A scene which continues across two pages, usually in the coloured centre of British comics.

Story Twist

Unexpected plot development.

Strip

A shortened way of saying comic strip.

Sunday Page

Appears in American newspapers, a strip series that only appears on Sundays (occasionally taking up a full page), or the continuation of a newspaper strip that has appeared throughout the week. Sunday pages are always in colour.

Swipe

Some naughty artists, usually beginners, imitate, or even trace, a piece of artwork by another artist. Frowned on in the profession, but still appears quite regularly in American comic books.

Syndicate

Organisations that will try to sell your newspaper strip to newspapers in other countries. They take a percentage, but can make you a lot more money.

Thought Balloon

Useful device to show what a character is thinking. The balloon is scalloped with small bubbles linking it to a character's head.

Through-(A Character's)-Eyes

Art direction. You want the reader to see what the character sees through his or her eyes.

Title

Not to be confused with LOGO. Refers to the title of the individual story.

Vignette

A comic strip panel with softened, misty edges.

Visuals

The drawings in a comic strip.

Underground

Comics which are published by 'alternative' publishers and feature controversial topics, portrayed graphically, such as bizarre sex practises, the taking of drugs, political statements, which are free from censorship. The undergrounds started in the American era of Flower Power; they are still published but the best work has long since been done. There is little scope for the scriptwriter who wishes to make money from comics writing — most underground writers and artists would probably claim they aren't interested in making money. They are only interested in making statements about our society.

Weekly

A comic that is published every seven days.

Wide Angle/Wide Panel

Art direction. A panel that is wider than the average. A wide panel is useful for depicting a powerful scene, such as an army of soldiers waiting for the call into battle, etc.

Worm's-Eye View

Looking up from a lower elevation.

Appendix Two

Sound Effects

There's nothing like a good sound effect to make a comic story that much
more exciting. Where would our characters be without custard pies going
SPLAATT! in their faces, being blown up with a BANG!, or getting hit on
the head with a delicious DONG! So here, for all you writers who are
stuck for *the* word, is . . .

Creative Imaginations Guide to Comic Words!

BOINK!
PLOP!
WHIZZZ!
PLUMMP!
GLLOPPP!
WHOOOSSSHHH!
THUMP! THUMPA! THUMP!
HOOOOOSSHH!
SSSSQUEEELCH!
SPLOOOT!
KAAA-BAAAAAM!
SLUURRRP!
RRRUUUUMMMMMBLE!
ZZZZZAAAAAPPPP!
KER-FLUMP!
KOCKETY KNOCKETY KNOCK!
SPLLUUUUUUUURRRRGGGH!
KRRAACCK!
VROOOM!
COUGH!
SPLUT!
KACHUGGG!
KACHUSHH!
KAGOINK!
BLEEP!
BZZZZT!
PLUNK!
TWOYNNNG!
SNAP!
FSSSSHHHH!

120

KOFF!
KLUNK!
KLANG!
SKKKREEEEEEEEETCH!
SKKRROOOOOOOONNNKCH!
SCHRRIINNNNNNNNNNNK!
BU-BU-BU-BUMP!
SPLOOODGEE!
BUZZ!
PHWEEEEEEEEEP!
GLOMPH!
DONK!
GRAB!
CRACKLE!
FLASH!
PFFFT!
CLONK!
TUG!
BBBRRRIIINNNNNGGG!
CLIP! CLOP!
VARRROOOM!
DOOOONNNG!
JAM!
JAB!
SPLURGLE!
BLLOOOOOSSSSH!
BLAZOIINNGGG!
SQUEAK!
CRUNCH!
CHEW!
SLOBBER!
CRRRRUUMMMMMBLE!
BUUUURRRRRP!
WHACK!
HURL!
SPLUDGE!
SLIP!
SLITHER!
WOP-BOPPA-LOOBA-AND-A-WOP-BAM-BOO!
FLIBBEDY-FLOP!
FATOOOOM!
PLUDD!
CRACKKA-CRACKKA-CRAK!
FUMMPP!
PLODD!
FLUMMPHH!
HMMPH!
NEEEEEOOOOOOWWW!
NEE-NER!

BUBBLE-BUBBLE!
HA, HA!
OOOOEEER!
YEUCH!
YEEOOOWCHH!
ARF! ARF!
WOOF!
SCREEEECCCHH!
WHUMMP!
WALLOP!
GURGLE!
GLUG! GLUG!
KABLOOEY!
YIPES!
KERSPLATTT!
HAW, HAW!
HAR, HAR!
HEE, HEE!
CACKLE! CLACKLE!
CREEEAK!
CRASH!
CRRAAASSSSSH!
KRASH!
KRRAAASSSH!
SPLASH!
SPERLASH!
SPLOSH!
SPLOOOSSSH!
WHACK!
THUDD!
SLICE!
WHOMP!
FWOPP!
SLAP!
BOOP!
BEEP! BADOOP!
CLANG!
ZOOOM!
BONNG!
BOING!
BLOIP!
PRANG!
SMAAASSSH!
POOF!
SPRONG!
SLAM!
KABONNG!
DONG!
KRAK!

CREAK!
CREESH!
ZZZIIIP!
FRAK!
FRABAM!
SCRECK!
FWOOOSSH!
CRIP!
FLIP!
SWWWIIISH!
FWOOM!
BERRAM!
POP!
PHTZZZZT!
ZAAAAAAK!
PHOOOM!
WUUUMMMPH!
???!!
FOOSH!
FASHOOOM!
KRAAA-AK!
SHHRAAAK!
MMMMMMMMMM!
SKKKKKRRRTTZZZ!
CLICK!
JIIOOONG!
WHUMPH!
DINGALINGALING!
KER-SPLOOOSSSH!
ZZZZZZ!
PING!
ZIPP!
BANG!
HISSSS!

Appendix Three

There are a number of useful addresses for the comic writer to have at hand. These range from comic companies, and comic news magazines, to comic shops and dealers. The list can never be fully comprehensive because magazines are cancelled and companies go out of business more or less continuously. However, the following list is as up-to-date as we can get, and includes our own favourites.

British Comic Companies

D. C. Thomson & Co, Ltd

Albert Square
Dundee   or
DD1 9QJ

Courier Street
Meadowside
Dundee
DD1 9QJ

Fleetway Publications
Irwin House
118 Southwark Street
London
SE1 0SW

London Editions, Ltd
PO Box 111
Egmont House
Manchester
M60 3BL

Marvel Comics, Ltd
Arundel House
13-15 Arundel Street
London
WC2R 3ED

Suron International Publications
44 Hill Street
London
W1X 8LB

TV Times Publications Ltd
195 Knightsbridge
London
SW7 1RS

Book-Cassette Companies

Rainbow Communications
Friese Green House
7 Chelsea Manor Street
London
SW3 3TW

Tempo Books
Multiple Sound Holdings
3 Standard Road
Park Royal Industrial Estate
London
NW10 6EY

American Comic Companies

Comico The Comic Company
1547 DeKalb St
Norristown
PA
19401

DC Comics Inc
666 Fifth Avenue
New York
N.Y.
10103

Eclipse Comics
Box 1099
Forestville
CA
95436

First Comics Inc
435 N. LaSalle St
Chicago
IL
60610

Marvel Comics Ltd
387 Park Ave. South
New York
NY
10016

Organisations

The Society of Strip Illustration (SSI)
7 Dilke Street
London
SW3 4JE

Comic News Magazines

There are a number of comic news magazines published in America, but in our opinion none tops Britain's own news magazine: SPEAKEASY. This is a monthly, newspaper-style publication that features the most important comic news. It includes information regarding who's publishing, writing, and drawing what comics, the comics just arriving on the bookstands, comics that have been delayed or cancelled, feature articles on popular new titles, and all the latest news in the entire field of British, American, and European comics. Full details from:

Speakeasy
18 Trelawn Road
London
W2 1DJ

Comic Shops

Shops that specialise in the sales of British, American and European comics, and related items. There are over 50 such shops in Britain, the best, of course, being in and around London.

Comic Showcase
76 Neal St
London
WC2

Mega City
18 Inverness St
Camden Town
London
NW1

Virgin Megastore
14-16 Oxford St
London
W1

Virgin Megastore
98 Corporation St
Birmingham

Virgin Megastore
157-161 Western Rd
Brighton

Comic Showcase
19/20 St Clements St
Oxford

Forbidden Planet
Denmark St
London

Comic Dealers

If you can't get to a comic shop, you can buy comics through the post, from one of the many dozens of comic dealers. For a SAE, they will be happy to send you their latest lists. Four of our favourites are listed below.

Fantasy Collector
94 Westover Road
Hall
Broadstairs
Kent
CT10 3EX

Gaggle of Games
The Liberty Shopping
Basildon Town Centre
Basildon
Essex

Just Comics
2 Crossmead Avenue
Greenford
Middlesex
UB6 9TY

John Dakin
7 Cross Court
Denmark Hill
London
SE5

Fanzines

For those of you who still feel you would like a chance to practise the craft of comic scriptwriting before attempting to sell scripts professionally, there are a number of magazines published by comic fans. These are known as 'fanzines.' They are a wonderful training ground for the would-be writer. (One of us actually started our writing career this way.) There is no payment for work, but it does allow you to learn the trade without the worry of feeling that your first failed script will be your last. There is only one fanzine we can recommend wholeheartedly, one that has been around for over ten years. The editor, Geoff Lamprey, is always interested in talented new writers for the magazine. The address is:

The X-Men Fan Club
74 Gloucester Road
Bridgwater
Somerset
TA6 6EA